BOOK REVIEWING

BOOK
REVIEWING

Edited by Sylvia E. Kamerman
Editor, *The Writer*

A guide to writing book reviews for newspapers, magazines, radio, and television—by leading book editors, critics, and reviewers

Boston THE WRITER, INC. *Publishers*

"Reviewer's Dues," by L. E. Sissman, is reprinted by
permission. Copyright © 1974 by Anne Sissman.

Library of Congress Cataloging in Publication Data

Main entry under title:
Book reviewing.
    1. Book reviewing—Addresses, essays, lectures.
I. Kamerman, Sylvia E.
PN98.B7B6   808'.066'0281   78-9390
ISBN 0-87116-113-3

Printed in the United States of America

FOREWORD

WITH MORE than 40,000 new books published each year in the United States, no reader, however enthusiastic, can possibly read more than a small percentage of them. Readers and book buyers have to depend upon the judgment of competent book reviewers to guide them in the selection of their reading.

For those who wish to learn the craft of book reviewing, there are specific steps that can be taken in criticizing or making an appraisal of a book. Certain basic do's and don'ts can be mastered, and with practice the skills will be sharpened, as will the reviewer's critical judgment. A reviewer should love books and reading and should read as much as possible in a variety of fields, to enrich his or her knowledge and to provide an authoritative basis of judgment. Reviewers should enjoy browsing in libraries and bookstores; in the local library, the big-city library or university or special library; in second-hand bookstalls and book counters in antique shops. To be a good reviewer you must be drawn to books, whenever and wherever they are available for reading or leafing through. And usually reviewers *care* about how books come into being, who creates them (the authors), who edits, plans and produces them (the publishers), and who sells them (the bookstores) or displays them (libraries as well as stores).

Aspiring reviewers should be familiar with a broad range of book review columns, sections, and pages in various types of publications, magazines and newspapers. If novice reviewers can train their minds to see bits of information about authors, books and the publishing world in these book pages and in other newspapers and magazines, so much the better. This kind of rich background is bound to filter into their reviews and make them more readable and publishable. As this happens, a reviewer's reputation may grow, and readers will come to rely upon him for sound judgments and guidance.

Book reviewing may be full time, part time, intermittent, occasional; it may be a vocation or an avocation. Learning the basic skills of book reviewing will enable average readers to get the most from a book. Book reviewing should be done with intellectual courage and honesty; enthusiasm and a sense of proportion and balance are required.

Qualities of a review

A book review should help the reader decide whether or not he or she wants to read the book. Readers have a right to expect informed judgment of the book as well as an appreciation of its literary quality. There is no room for hostility (against the author or the subject) or for personal prejudices based on extraneous factors that may distort a reviewer's judgment. There should be some code of ethics, explicit or implied, that guides book reviewers in giving opinions, so that they do not simply attack what they happen not to like or understand. Reviewers should be as fair as possible in saying how well the author has carried out his or her intent in the book being reviewed, and they should judge the book that has been written, not the book they wish the author had written.

If a reviewer has a strong bias on the subject of the book, pro or con, he or she should acknowledge that bias at the outset. Often a strong bias in a review will discourage a reader from reading a book in which he would otherwise be interested. The wide range of opinion about the same book often seen in reviews by competent reviewers in prestigious journals or newspapers (and even in the daily as opposed to the Sunday book section of the same newspaper) points up the difficulties of overstating an opinion of a book—unless such opinion can be well supported by specific references and quotations from the book.

The fame or notoriety of the author or the topic may influence a reviewer, as may advance publicity, a local tie-in to a celebrity, and even a publication date that coincides with some major event—such as, increasingly, movie and TV tie-ins.

In some cases, the book editor assigns a book to an unsuitable reviewer—for example, one who may look down on books written "only for entertainment." A reviewer who does not like mystery and suspense fiction may assess such a book by subjective, arbitrary standards (despite the fact that millions of readers read such books exclusively, with pleasure and satisfaction) without saying how well the author fulfilled his intent, how the book measures up to other books in the same field, and whether or not the book is well written —as many novels of this kind are.

Reviewers should not use the printed word to air their

frustrations or disappointments. They should also avoid making statements that appear to be written with the express intent of being quoted in an advertisement for the book in such high-circulation newspapers as *The New York Times*.

Types of reviews

Book reviewing is far from an exact science: It reflects the background, education, training, biases, enthusiasms, and even the state of mind of the reviewer at the time he or she reads and analyzes a book. Also, the medium in which a book review appears can determine the style, length, and depth of a review. In *The New York Review of Books*, a review will often be a long essay that discusses the book in detail and also covers an entire genre of writing. *Time*, *Newsweek* and similar publications will often tie a book to the current literary or political scene—although they publish only three or four reviews a week. The review will sometimes appear outside the regular book review pages in a section on Modern Living, Behavior, Science, Education, or in the department that suits the field covered by the book.

The New York Times Book Review uses essay reviews to discuss broad literary areas, but for the most part uses fairly short critical reviews. Magazines like *The New Yorker* and *The Atlantic* will often publish a long essay or article about an individual book and related subjects. Almost all other newspapers and magazines use short reviews, but even these incorporate some appraisal and description of the books.

Various kinds of book coverage are known as reviews:

The straight descriptive review—usually little more than the vital statistics of title, author, price, publisher, and a one-line description—which is often staff written, and involves no value judgment. This is not a review in the real sense, since there is no evaluation by the reviewer, only a summary of what is in the book.

A short review of a few paragraphs can convey the flavor of a book, mentioning the major and minor characters, summarizing the plot or storyline (without giving away the solution of a mystery or the denouement of a dramatic plot), and stating in the final sentence or two how well the book is done and whether or not the reviewer would recommend it.

The essay review describes the book more fully, compares it to other books by the author and to books of the same type by other authors, and explicitly or indirectly states the reviewer's opinion of the book. There is also the critique, which goes beyond the essay to discuss a whole genre, a literary movement, and the entire body of the author's work, setting the new book into this literary context or framework.

A long and detailed review may be required for a novel by a well-known writer, with a description of the period in which it is set, and any special circumstances that will enhance reader interest. The earlier works of the author may be mentioned and compared. In this type of essay review, the reviewer can include material that will direct the readers' attention to other authors, indicating always the quality of the writing in the book under discussion and how it measures up to other books and authors mentioned. This requires continuous "writer-watching," to help a reviewer keep up to date with events in the book world.

As a reviewer, you must work to achieve fairness, objectivity, accuracy, and sensitivity in your reviews. To accomplish this, you need not be an authority or specialist; through constant reading in ever-widening areas you can cultivate a rich literary background that will make your opinions respected by readers. Aiming for this kind of credibility is an absolute necessity if you are to grow and develop as a reviewer whose judgment will serve as an informal reader's guide. As Eliot Fremont-Smith, Book Editor of *The Village Voice*, has said, "A critic writes for history; a reviewer writes, for the most part, for the current promotion of books, as a 'consumer's guide.'"

The chapters that follow have been contributed by leading reviewers and book editors, whose experience reflects a broad range of special fields and styles of reviewing. It is my belief that the advice and suggestions of these eminent critics will be stimulating and valuable to aspiring book reviewers.

—S. E. K.

CONTENTS

INTRODUCTION

To BECOME a book reviewer you must care about books, and reading must be an important part of your life and world. You must be willing to delve into the background of an author or a field of writing to enrich your knowledge and feel for a person or period or place. You must have a talent for writing clear, persuasive prose that will give an accurate picture of the book under discussion, and a sense of fairness and responsibility to author and reader to do this in a balanced, objective way.

Even when all of these qualifications are met, however, it is important for you as a would-be reviewer to know the practical side of breaking into book reviewing, the range of opportunities that exist for the reviewer, and the basics of getting started.

At the outset, you should survey the publications in your area that use book reviews. Become familiar with the local daily or weekly newspapers, and explore the monthly city or regional magazines. Your most important hurdle is to convince an editor to give you a chance at reviewing one or more books. That may not be as difficult as it seems, since most publications cannot afford full-time staff reviewers and depend for reviews either on the individual free-lance reviewer or sometimes on syndicated reviewing services. After analyzing a local publication, write a half-dozen book reviews you have reason to think the editor might use, and submit them for publication and as samples of your work. (At this early stage you may have to get the books yourself or borrow them from the library. Later as an established reviewer you can request review copies from the book editor.) If you present reviews of books on local history, a novel or other book by a local author, a biography of a person who lived in your area and still may have descendants there, a cookbook by a local restaurateur—your reviews are likely to capture the interest and attention of an editor, even one who has never used book reviews or who has not used them on a regular basis.

Once you have succeeded in getting several reviews accepted and published in a local or regional newspaper or magazine, you may want to approach some larger and more widely read magazines and newspapers that have their editorial offices in or near the city where you live. There are thousands of publications—mass market magazines, newspapers, popular magazines—that take short, lively, well-written reviews, and a smaller number of specialized publications (technical, scientific, professional, academic) that are interested in reviews by specialists or experts in their respective fields. If you have knowledge of computers, teaching, energy, family therapy, housing, urban problems, or money management, for example, you could certainly approach one of the magazines or newspapers in your field and suggest a review of a book that would be of particular interest to its readers. All of these publications would, of course, expect judgment of the value of the book, and your expertise would give your review the kind of credibility an editor would want.

There are other ways you can get a start as a reviewer: Many organizations present book reviews as a program at their meetings. The women's-club circuit has been the launching pad for many regional and local reviewers, who got started by giving a review of one or more books at meetings of these clubs, or at such groups as the P.T.A., Monday lunch clubs, and the like. Program chairmen may be interested in having entertaining book reviews at some of their meetings. Such cultural or literary programs for an organization require you to select the right book or books, and it is important to know the kind and size of your audience in making that selection. It may be that there are two or three books presenting different views of a subject that can be reviewed together on such a program.

Incidentally, preparing reviews of a group of books about a central theme or subject, or of the same literary type, is often worthwhile, as you will note in the group reviews that appear in the major newspapers and magazines. Thus, a group of short reviews—of mystery and suspense novels, poetry, biographies about the same person, books for children, anthologies of short stories, historical romances, science fiction, or whatever—is often presented as a "cluster review" under a single heading.

Another possible training ground for aspiring reviewers, although a limited one, is the local radio station or television channel. Occasionally the program director of the station may be willing to allow a local reviewer to give a one-to-five-minute book review of one or more books. Obviously, such reviews require concise, compressed writing, in which the feel and flavor of the books are conveyed quickly. This is excellent training for making every word count and saying what you mean, and while this is probably one of the more difficult places in which to get a start, it could be a good proving ground.

Getting the books

Having advance information about forthcoming books and, if possible, an advance copy of a book in time to write your review of it before its publication date may be the key to placing your reviews. As a rule, unless you are an established reviewer or a specialist in a field, you will not be able to get free advance review copies of books. However, newspapers and magazines with regular book review pages or columns receive advance copies of most books of general interest directly from the publishers, and you may be able to get an editor to assign certain of these books to you for review. Timely books or those on which there has been a good deal of advance publicity may be assigned to more experienced reviewers. But bear in mind that most books do not fall into this group, and beginners may have many opportunities to review other books.

The smaller local papers or specialized publications do not receive review copies regularly. You should therefore get as much information as possible about the books that are going to be published and then on your own get copies of the books you want to review for such a publication.

If you have had several reviews published, you can write to book publishers requesting advance review copies of books. Such a letter should be addressed to the publicity director of the company (you will find these names and addresses in *Literary Market Place*). These letters should be typed, using the letterhead of a newspaper or publication for which you review. Here is a sample letter:

Ms. Jane Doe, Publicity Director
Doubleday & Co., Inc.
245 Park Ave.
New York, New York 10017

Dear Ms. Doe:

Will you please send me an advance copy of your forth-coming title, *Life of Benjamin Franklin*, by John Roe, for possible review in *The Center City Gazette*.

This book should be of special interest to the *Gazette's* readers, and I'm eager to bring it to their attention. I will be glad to send you two copies of the review when published.

Sincerely yours,
Ruth Smith

To get advance publicity information about forthcoming books, you need a wide range of sources. You should regularly consult *Publishers Weekly*, a magazine available at most libraries, to find out what books are scheduled for publication in the months ahead. Another source of information may be the book publishing companies themselves. You can write to the publicity directors of these companies asking to be put on the mailing list for catalogues and publicity releases about books and authors. Also say that you are planning to review a specific book on their list, naming the publication in which the review may appear. You might include something about your background when you make such requests for publicity material, thus establishing your credentials for receiving further information or review copies of specific books. You will find addresses of book publishing companies in *Publishers Weekly*, *Literary Market Place*, *The Writer* Magazine, and *The Writer's Handbook*.

The value of the material you will receive once you get on publishers' publicity lists is immeasurable, since you will have information about books and authors that readers always find fascinating and that will greatly enrich the reviews you write. Human-interest anecdotes about the writing of the book, the author or the subject of a biography provide you with invaluable material that can establish you as a colorful and competent writer.

As a beginning reviewer, you will have to convince the editors that you are qualified to write reviews for them on a general or specific type of book. If you succeed, editors will be more likely to assign to you titles they feel you can handle.

At first you may get no payment, except for the copy of the book you review. After a time, there may be some small per-review payment, but this is usually modest, except in the case of reviewers on important newspapers or nationally known magazines. Of course, the regular established staff reviewers, full- or part-time, are well paid for their individual reviews or regular columns.

Who is your audience?

Knowing who will read your reviews is important, since it can help determine the emphasis of your review and the points you may wish to make. This does not mean that you will change your judgment of the quality of a book to suit your audience, but if you are writing a review for a publication that has a strong political focus, you may couch your comments in terms of that particular focus. Similarly, if you are reviewing a book on science, you will comment on not only the accuracy and importance of the book as a scientific volume but also whether it is for the layman or the professional. You would review the same book on one level in a magazine or paper of general circulation and quite differently in a magazine of sociology, urban affairs, medicine, or any other specialized field.

People read reviews for various purposes:

a) As a guide to book selection. Librarians may use reviews to help them make their choice of books to purchase. General readers will base their book buying and reading on reviews.

b) As a way of keeping up with literature and writing, through those reviewers who provide such information.

c) As the basis for choosing books for others. This is common in all fields, but especially so in the case of children's books, because children rarely if ever select the books that are published for them. Librarians choose the books for the libraries from which young readers get most of their books, and teachers select the titles for supplementary reading in the classroom or school library. Parents and others who give books to children also determine what children read. Hence, reviews of bcoks for children are extremely influential in determining what gets onto library shelves and what provides the personal reading of children at home. The burden on the reviewer, therefore, is to review books for young people in terms of their world and in terms of the values the books may illustrate, and to provide as broad a base as possible for the future reading habits of children.

Fundamentals

Although there will be wide variation in the style, content, tone, length, and emphasis of a review, whether it is a short appraisal of a hundred words or less, or an essay, feature review or literary critique, certain elements should be included in every review.

Obviously, what could be called "vital statistics" about a book must be included:

- Title, author, publisher, price, paperback or hardcover, length, illustrated or translated.
- Indication of the type of material—fiction, nonfiction, essays, poetry, drama, biography, fine arts, science, architecture, juvenile, mystery, etc.

In addition, reviews often include the following:

- General description of the contents of the book and purpose.
- Information about the author that is relevant or interesting.
- If this is a first novel or book of poetry, note if the author has previously written short material for magazines, journals, or specialized publications.
- If not a *first* novel, state how this new book compares with the author's earlier works—or possibly with novels on the same theme. For example, if you are reviewing a novel about adolescence or the loneliness of prisoners, the tragedy of aging athletes, etc., and there is another new work of fiction on the same theme, you might wish to comment on the relative quality of both novels. A book of poems may be compared to other collections of poetry, and two biographies about the same person would be worth some comment.
- Scope of book and author's special qualifications to write it.
- Indicate how well the author has realized his intent or fulfilled the purpose of the book. Although this judgment is essential, you must make sure your opinion does not overshadow the discussion of the book itself.
- Comment on the style and writing in the book.
- Write your reviews in a lively and readable, even anecdotal style. In other words, a review—even a short one—should be good reading on its own.
- Accuracy is essential in writing a review, from the correctness

of the name of the book and author (with no misspellings!) to any quotations from the book. There are often letters in the book sections of magazines and newspapers from authors who take issue with a reviewer for misquotation.

Preparing the review

Before attempting to break into a particular newspaper or magazine as a reviewer, be sure to study the reviews published in that publication for style, tone, emphasis, length.

Here are some specific steps that beginners may find useful in writing reviews:

1. Read the book, noting in the margin passages you may want to refer to in your review, or to quote. There is usually a limitation of three hundred words a reviewer may quote without infringement of copyright; request permission from the publisher if you want to quote more. When actually writing the review, you can quickly refer to your marginal notations or underlined examples of an author's style, tendency to repeat certain words or phrases, or relevant sentences that will illustrate the points you are making in the review.

2. Sometimes you may wish to read through a book first to get the flavor, and then go back to make notes in the margin, underline some short or longer sections, or take notes so that you will not have to trust your memory, especially when you plan to quote.

3. Outline the points you wish to make in the review, and make notes of the overall impression you have of how well the author has achieved what he or she set out to do.

4. Consider the publication you are writing for: its audience, emphasis (for layman or specialist), and whether it is a trade journal, a daily newspaper, or a book page or section.

5. Try to find a theme or news tie-in or angle that you can use to give unity and coherence to the review and to gear it to your readership.

6. Do a rough draft of the review along the lines of your theme or angle.

7. Go over the review, sentence by sentence, word by word, to polish, refine, prune, and to make sure you have said what you intended in the best way you can.

8. Retype your review on 8½" x 11" paper, double space, or in a prescribed format required by the paper or magazine.

9. Reread carefully for typos, last-minute changes or corrections in wording. Retype if necessary and send your review off to the editor.

10. Keep copies of the review as submitted and as published. There may be cuts and editorial changes in the review as printed, and you can learn a great deal about the requirements for reviewing for that particular publication from studying these changes.

Also . . .

- Be sure that you do not miss deadlines when submitting to a book section, weekly newspaper or magazine.

- Send the publicity department of the book publisher two copies of your published reviews. This courtesy will help you greatly in getting more books to review in the future.

Getting started

To help you get started, you may find it useful to try to answer some of the questions that follow. Jot down your answers, and you will have the basic material for your review. You will have to rearrange this material, but answering these questions may help you find the angle or theme for your review and the phrase or sentence for a lead that will capture the reader's attention at once. You can also fill in quotations and other references and comments from the book that you jotted down in your notes. If you are writing a very short review, you will have to do some cutting, but the basic material will be there.

Questions your review may try to answer:

Fiction

- Does the novel illuminate a whole level of society, a period in history, or a city, country or region most modern readers are probably unfamiliar with?

- Do the hero and other characters live the kinds of lives with which readers can or would like to identify?

- Is the intent of the novel primarily serious or light, entertaining or didactic, romantic or realistic, negative or optimistic in outlook?

- Is the author expressing through his characters and plot some important theme or social ideal? If it is a political novel, does it reflect the seamy side of politics, or simply the excitement of being on the inside? Is it a novel about power and control by elected officials? Is the tone cynical or approving?

- Does the novel observe or describe real life, striving for a quality of naturalism and lifelikeness? This type of fiction writing—sometimes called "slice of life"—is the core of many successful modern novels.

- Is this a *roman à clef* (a novel in which real persons—and sometimes events—appear thinly disguised with fictitious names)?

- Is the book well edited, in that it is not overwritten and needlessly long, or, if long, is its length justified by the scope of the plot, theme, and characters?

- Are the characters and the period of the book presented in a way that seems real to the reader?

- Is this a book for the mass audience or for the more discriminating, limited audience for books in the literary tradition—or for both?

- Does the reader want to turn the page and continue reading to see how the writer will develop and resolve his characters' dilemmas, problems, conflicts, and goals? Or is the novel essentially boring? Is the solution credible and satisfying?
- Are the characters and storyline worthy of the theme—and vice versa?
- Is there some aspect of the characterization, plot, theme or style that is unusual in conception or treatment, adding to or detracting from the overall effectiveness and success of the book, and adding to or detracting from the reader's pleasure and satisfaction? Give examples.
- What part does the setting play in the effectiveness of the novel? Is it used to reinforce the characterization and plot, or does it serve as a foil for the character and a goad to action and decisions?
- Does the author successfully convey the desired emotional reactions to his readers?

In reviewing certain types of novels, there are special taboos:

In mystery fiction, for example, the plot must *never* be revealed. There are some novels promoted as general works of fiction that could be included in the mystery-suspense genre, and in these, the plot element is very strong, so that it must not be given away by implied or explicit summary statements. Since entertainment and reader satisfaction are the goal of most fiction, knowing the outcome of the plot in advance will not only destroy that potential pleasure, but will also make the reading of the book in some cases seem superfluous.

Nonfiction

When you review nonfiction books, the following specific points should be covered:

- How is the author qualified to write this nonfiction book? Academic experience? Political experience (federal, state, or local level)? Special accomplishments or work in the field (for example, CIA agent, former ambassador)?

- Source material—personal, primary, secondary?

- Time, style, point of view.

- Author's purpose and conclusion; evaluation by reviewer.

- Illustrations (photographs, charts, maps).

- Quotations (not too long) to support your points in the review.

- Is the book for the lay reader or a special audience? Can it be understood and enjoyed by both groups, though for different reasons?

- Does this book stem from or illuminate any news events (as in the case of the numerous books on Watergate)?

- In a biography, does the book seem to be comprehensive, including the negative as well as the positive aspects of the subject's life? Is it on the whole favorable to the subject, or harsh, trying to show him or her in the worst possible light? Is the subject of the book living? Does the biographer state or imply any bias, and not pretend to be objective? Does he overstate the subject's successes and underplay his weaknesses? Does the biography seem to be fictionalized to the degree that the author invents material when facts are not easily available? Is the book readable and lively, giving the reader a picture of the person as he or she lived? Does the biographer convey a conviction about the subject so that the reader feels that he really knows what the subject was like, and the motivation for his behavior? How does this biography compare with others about the same person or period? ·Is the subject or the time in which he or she lived the most important part of the book?

- Is there an attempt in a biography or historical book, for example, to create an authentic picture of the period, the place, the events, and the people of that time? How well does the author succeed?

How authentic is the documentation the author provides (or does not provide) in the form of letters, diaries, journals, newspaper articles, new documents that other biographers or historians did not use or did not have access to? For example, in a book about Alger Hiss, author-historian Allen Weinstein was able to consult and analyze FBI documents and files previously unavailable and to have interviews with five Russians who were in the Russian Intelligence Service at the time. All of this is reflected in his book *Perjury: The Hiss-Chambers Case.*

As stated by biographer Leon Edel, the biographer's imagination must be used in putting the materials together, but "he must not imagine the materials." The past must be totally understood and absorbed by the author, and then presented in readable and believable form for the reader. There is, of course, some discretion and therefore possible bias on the part of the writer in the emphasis used and the way facts are selected and presented. Consequently, the truth is elusive, and nonfiction reviewers must try to assess the degree to which the author realized it.

It is particularly important in reviewing nonfiction to present clearly the area of the period or life or historical sequence of events or political happenings that the author covers in the book—and to judge the book on that basis. While a reviewer may wish the author had chosen another time or emphasis or set of events, the reviewer should note this only to the degree that the omission of certain materials may have distorted the picture presented.

Summary

Book reviewing can be an excellent place to start your career as a writer and to become acquainted with a wide range of local and regional as well as national and mass-market publications. Some small magazines and papers may publish your reviews, and, with good reader response, may make reviews a permanent part of their editorial content. Developing a specialty often results from reading at random and finding that there is a pattern in the type of book you like best. The more you then read in that narrower (but not narrow!) area, the richer the store of information you have to draw on in your reviewing—and this is bound to impress editors, as well as readers, with your competence. Your qualifications may come to the editor's mind as new titles in your field are to be assigned for review.

—Sylvia E. Kamerman

BOOK REVIEWING

ROBERT KIRSCH is an author, teacher, and critic. He is daily book reviewer and literary critic for *The Los Angeles Times*, has taught critical and creative writing at UCLA and other universities, and has written eleven books—novels and works of nonfiction. A collection of his reviews and essays—*Lives, Works, and Transformations*—was published by Capra Press to mark his twenty-five years of daily book reviewing.

1

The Importance of Book Reviewing

by ROBERT KIRSCH

THERE ARE no simple formulas for book reviewing. Like most writing, effects can be achieved in many different ways, depending on audience, medium, subject. What I will try to do here is alert the aspiring book reviewer to some of the processes and values I have found useful in twenty-five years of daily book reviewing.

At its core, the book review is superior cultural reporting. It can be more than this, of course; it is most frequently less. One value the book reviewer and the literary critic must share is an accurate evocation of the work discussed. That seems easy. It isn't. The reviewer should convey to the reader the *news* of the book, the who, what, where, when, and how of the book, and the why. Very often this information is more important to the reader than your judgment on the worth of the book. Praise or blame doesn't mean much without communicating a sense of what the book is.

3

Try to let the book speak for itself as much as possible. It may be necessary to synopsize or paraphrase the author's material. But it is very helpful to the reader to be able to read a crucial passage, directly quoted. This gives the reader not only important information but a sense of the writer's style.

Read the book. This would seem understood, taken for granted. But many reviewers simply plunder a book for material to support a review they have already begun to shape as they read. With such a *set*, the review is bound to be unfair to the book and certainly unfair to the reader of the review. The bottom line for any criticism of the arts is *presence at the performance.* Skipping or skimming can change the impression a reviewer receives. Give the book a chance to make its point or at least to make it clear that it isn't worth your trouble. The speed of reading is not as important as the attention paid.

Respond to the book. Reading is not a passive experience. Reviewing is a critical activity. That is, informed judgments are expected of a reviewer. Reflection, thoughtful and judicious assessments are possible if you get some distance from the material. I find that the unconscious mind is very helpful in this regard. After reading, give the book some time to compel and mellow down response. An immediate review after reading, I have found, is more likely to be either unfairly deprecating or extravagant in its praise.

Declare your interest or bias. This may be the most important point in this piece. The worst thing a reviewer can do—because it is deceitful or hypocritical—is to assume a magisterial or detached style when in fact he knows and hates or envies the writer, knows and admires the writer, is a friend of the writer, or a colleague, fellow alumnus, or is married to the writer's sister. With rare exceptions I do not review any writers who are personal friends. When I do, I make this clear in the review. Every known and relevant bias should be expressed. I don't like stories about talking dogs or novels set in Florida. I don't know why. Generally I try to avoid reviewing these. But if I do, I let people know.

Learn who you are, what value systems you follow. This is the hardest requirement. When I teach critical writing, I often ask students to write their critical credo as the term begins. Most often, these are undigested, unexamined, and often confused renderings of what they have been told in literature courses, or of what they think literate, cultivated, tasteful people believe. Very few will start with their subjective responses to performance and reading, for they are usually embarrassed to say, "I like it," or "I don't like it." The fact is that all criticism has its ultimate roots in the subjective response, in pleasure or boredom. We may go on to develop or refine taste, critical theories, knowledge about the functions of art, broad erudition in works of the past; we may place works in context, discern influence, predict importance and greatness. But all of this must come after the subjective response. Then, we can say, "I like it, and this is why. . . ." Or, "I dislike it, and this is why. . . ."

This sense in each of us is what contributes to the notion of the *consensus gentium,* the standard of worth which Aristotle saw as the ultimate critical test of greatness, the response of many individuals over a long period of time. The book reviewer may tell you what is worth reading tomorrow, but he shares with the literary critic the hope that he can sense what is fine and enduring as well.

What we are trying to achieve is not so much objectivity—certainly not a spurious objectivity—but, rather, distance, balance, fairness. Being straight with the reader and the writer is more important than wearing a mask of authority or expertness.

Be interesting and amusing and bright but not at the expense of the book reviewed. When I first started reviewing, a well-known novelist, Robert Nathan, told me that I wouldn't ever amount to much as a critic because I was too fair, too concerned with the book rather than my own reputation. "I can tell you how to become the best-known critic in America in six months," he said. "Kick the hell out of every book that comes along, good, bad or indifferent. There are a hundred words of attack and assault and negation— and all of them vivid—to every word of praise." I asked him whether he would want his books treated that way. "Of course not," he said.

Fair reviews can be clever and interesting. But they take work and attention. It is much easier to jump off on self-promoting, show-off pieces. And I find that much of the inferior reviewing is just an opportunity for failed writers or aspiring writers to indulge themselves.

Remember that the book business is not the same as literature. The explosive rise of literacy and the expansion of new media, the challenge of leisure and the American penchant for self-improvement have produced a very different publishing industry. The book business has become an extension of journalism, of show business, of fads and fashions. I think this is generally a healthy development. Anything that gets people reading, whether it is comic books, Gothics, pornographic novels, or self-help primers, is bound to recruit readers for higher quality books. That is why at the beginning of the paperback revolution I started a policy of reviewing paperbacks. Book dealers objected, saying that these could be bought in drugstores and supermarkets. A few years later, they were glad to be selling paperbacks. The habit of buying books is what counts. Among the thousands of books published yearly there are non-books, almost books, poor books, and good books. Many of them require only reportage. The number of enduring works is bound to be very small. Use adjectives of greatness and importance sparingly. Book reviewers should help to keep the language from being devalued. And we must not become extensions of the flack machines, or extensions of publicity and blurbs.

Serve the reader. He is the one who depends on you. He is the one who will know soon enough whether you are authentic and reliable or phony and pretentious. You owe fairness to the writer and the book, but your major constituent is the reader who will buy or borrow from the library the book you recommend.

Write short. Book editors are always fighting the battle of space. A reviewer who writes a pithy, readable, informative review, meets his deadlines, and alerts an editor to a really good book or one which is not worth wasting space on, will always have assignments.

Finally, a helpful suggestion from Samuel Johnson, whose test of a book is particularly valuable to a beginning reviewer and may do some good for an experienced one. He asked three questions: *What did the writer try to do? How well did he do it? Was it worth doing in the first place?* These are worth your attention.

SAMPLE REVIEW

[*I read* Reeling, *by Pauline Kael, about two weeks or more before writing the review. I never take notes on a book, though occasionally I will jot down an idea on a scrap of paper. I put slips of paper into the book to mark position of quotes or useful points.*

I like Pauline Kael's work and assign her I Lost It at the Movies *to my class in critical writing as an example of excellent reviewing. It seemed to me that she lost in* Reeling *some of her verve and perspective; it tends to be a little more quippy and magisterial. I tried to show some of the contradictions between what she said and what she did. But on balance, she is such a good reviewer that I said these things rather too subtly, more for getting them in rather than banging her on the head. That's my way.*

—R. K.

THE PASSIONATE MOVIEGOER
by Robert Kirsch, *Los Angeles Times* Book Critic

Reeling. By Pauline Kael (Atlantic-Little, Brown: $12.95.)

"Movies operate in a maze of borderlines; criticism is a balancing act, trying to suggest perspectives on the emotions viewers feel, trying to increase their enjoyment of movies without insulting their susceptibilities to simple, crude pop," Pauline Kael, film critic of *The New Yorker*, writes in the foreword to the collection of reviews and essays written between September, 1972, and April, 1975.

Sheer and increasing sensory impact, a kind of tribalized experience, the hangover of rock, has increased along with breakthroughs all along hitherto taboo areas. "So many images, sounds, and awakened memories may contribute to the film's effect on us that often we can't quite sort out what we think about the way we've been moved. We're not even sure sometimes if we liked it, but we certainly felt it."

For the critic who has to write about the experience of films in this far-out period, the challenge is tougher. And the reviews in this collection, immensely readable and among the most illuminating film criticism written in this country, reflect that difficulty. Some of them, notably her effusive piece on *Last Tango in Paris* ("a landmark in movie history . . .

The movie breakthrough has finally come . . ."), reflect the kind of exaggerated response she warns about in her foreword:

". . . When a movie has worked for people—startling them, like *The Towering Inferno,* or enlisting their sympathies and making them weep, like *Walking Tall,* or making them feel vindictive and sadistic, like the Charles Bronson film *Death Wish*—the hardest thing for a critic to do is to convince them that it isn't a work of art. It's almost impossible to persuade people that a shallow, primitive work can give them a terrific kick."

Breakthrough in sexuality

Yet, that is precisely what Miss Kael has done in the *Tango* review. The breakthrough mentioned above is in the area of sexuality. "Exploitation films have been supplying mechanized sex—sex as physical stimulant but without any passion or emotional violence." Miss Kael, discerning the power and truth of the book behind the script, was evidently so moved to see motivation and depth supplied that the exaggerations of Brando's performance and the nubile numbness of Maria Schneider, the pedestrian direction of Bertolucci, are elevated to greatness merely in contrast to the worst of this type of film. "This must be the most powerfully erotic movie ever made, and it may turn out to be the most liberating movie ever made . . ." is a statement which proves that even a fine critic can go haywire.

But this is an exception. Most of the reviews and essays, including the controversial "On the Future of Movies," as cutting a dissection of the Hollywood entrepreneurs and their captive artists as we have had, are an attempt at balance and perspective. Her victims may argue with that. ("To lambaste a Ross Hunter production is like flogging a sponge"; "Doesn't it seem a little soon for Robert Redford to be presiding over his own mutation into a legend? I was still waiting for him to become a new kind of hip and casually smart screen actor, and he's already jumped into the mythic-man roles in which tired aging stars can vegetate profitably"; "The grandiosity of *The Trial of Billy Jack* suggests that it's a complete con, but it may not be fair to use lack of artistry as evidence of dishonesty.")

Scourge of the bosses

When the reviews and essays are put togther and read, Miss Kael emerges less as a sour, vengeful, highbrow scourge of businessmen bosses and corrupt directors and "the true modern sex appeal—success," than as a dedicated and even passionate moviegoer, one who wants people to do their best (and may even be a trifle overgenerous with those who try), who often displays a sinewy moral as well as aesthetic stan-dard, and who takes movies and their characters seriously (no other reviewer comes near her for this quality). She is deep, intelligent and persuasive. The movies are lucky to have her as a critic, and moviegoers even luckier.

The glib mediocrities she attacks, the wheeler-dealers she exposes, the heavy investors who fancy that she is threatening their profits in some property, may paste her picture on the dartboard target in Beverly Hills offices. But she is a credit to film criticism—any criticism—for she makes informed judgments, she connects performance with life, present ex-pression with the past, most often says more about art and life than some of the pretentious pictures she reviews.

CHRISTOPHER LEHMANN-HAUPT is Senior Daily Book Reviewer at *The New York Times*.

2

The Daily Newspaper
Book Review

by CHRISTOPHER LEHMANN-HAUPT

THE HARDEST part of writing book reviews for a newspaper is learning to use your space effectively. Both because there isn't much of it available and because you have to grab the attention of a reader who is probably being distracted by the fact that his toast is burned, you simply cannot afford to write sentences or paragraphs that serve only a single purpose. Everything you write has to do double or even triple duty, as it were. It must convey information about the book being considered and, at the same time, express the reviewer's attitude toward that information.

Failure to do so is the most common mistake made by grade-school book-report writers and beginning book reviewers (which, of course, is what grade-school book-report writers actually are). For instance, the tendency of a third-grade reviewer of, say, "The Three Little Pigs" would be first to tell the story related in that well-known epic, and then to conclude by saying, "I liked this story very much, especially the part where the wolf fell into the pot of boiling water. It was exciting." But this is inefficient and boring, although no doubt to be forgiven in third-graders. The sentences describing the plot serve *only* to describe the plot, while the reviewer's attitude toward the story is confined to his concluding remarks. A reader of such a review would be forgiven for paying more attention to the toast than to the newspaper in which such an exercise appeared.

What experienced reviewers eventually learn to do is to convey information about the story while at the same time giving their opinions about it. Thus, a professional review of "The Three Little Pigs" might go as follows: "I was appalled by this story of the destruction of a member of a valued endangered species. It is all very well to celebrate the practicality of pigs by ennobling the porcine sibling who constructed his home out of bricks and mortar. But to wantonly destroy a wolf, even one with an excessive taste for porkers, is unconscionable in these ecologically critical times when both man and his domestic beasts continue to maraud the earth." And so on. As you see, the sentences are doing double duty.

If you now read over the accompanying review, "Cures for Illiteracy?" perhaps you will see what makes it tick. At the time it was written, I was teaching remedial writing at one of New York City's public colleges, which means, as anyone who has had a similar experience will doubtless understand, that I was in complete despair over teaching anyone to write and speak "correctly" by simply laying down the rules of proper grammar. At the same time, I had to concede the distinction and correctness of the two books under review, *Simple & Direct*, by Jacques Barzun, and *On Writing Well*, by William Zinsser. The form the review takes follows from the ambivalence of my feelings.

Thus, the game is given away in the very first sentence,

especially in the phrase, "I cannot finally fault . . ."—which is really to say, "I'm going to do a lot of faulting before I get through." In fact, if one had to write a single sentence expressing the attitude of the review—and incidentally any review of this length should be capable of being boiled down to a single coherent sentence—such a sentence might read, "While I cannot finally fault these two guides to writing better, I can find plenty wrong with them in the meantime."

As for the information conveyed in the review—that is, the description of the contents of the two books under discussion and the titles of other reference works that might be of use to writers: it is simply woven into the expression of those feelings, so to speak. This technique is most evident in the penultimate paragraph, where I have tried to relate my specific criticisms of the books to my general one by saying, ". . . even I, who should know better, began these books by feeling defensive. (I found myself jumping at Mr. Zinsser for writing. . . .)" The writing is doing double duty. It's as simple as that.

CURES FOR ILLITERACY?
by Christopher Lehmann-Haupt

Simple & Direct. A Rhetoric for Writers. By Jacques Barzun. 212 pages. Harper & Row. $10.

On Writing Well. An Informal Guide to Writing Nonfiction. By William Zinsser. 151 pages. Harper & Row. $6.95.

As someone who makes his living by putting words together, I cannot finally fault these two guides to writing better— one of them, *Simple & Direct,* a quasi-textbook by Jacques Barzun, who last year retired from a distinguished teaching career at Columbia University; the other, *On Writing Well,*

based on a course taught at Yale by the popular journalist
William Zinsser. Each of the books provides a useful check-
list of warnings and prescriptions—stop using the illogical
form of the adverb "hopefully" in such a sentence as "Hopefully, he will undertake the project hopefully"; look up the
true meaning of such words as "escalate" and "preempt"
before you misuse them in any more sentences; learn to distinguish between "repel" and "repulse," "precipitate" and
"precipitous," and "compose" and "comprise."

Each of the books confirms certain of my pet enthusiasms.
"I almost always urge people to write in the first person,"
says William Zinsser. "Writing is an act of ego and you might
as well admit it." (When I read this, I cheered.) How can you
understand the meanings of words without knowing their
roots? asks Mr. Barzun. And how can you understand the
roots of English words without knowing something of Latin
and Greek? (When I read this I found myself wishing again
that I hadn't slept through Caesar's "Commentaries on the
Gallic War.")

Why "no-no" is a no-no

Both of the books belong on any shelf of serious reference
works for writers—along with, say, Fowler's *Modern English
Usage,* Strunk and White's *The Elements of Style* and of
course as many different dictionaries of the English language
as you have money to buy and space to keep. For if you want
to know why "mindboggling" is a no-no (or, for that matter,
why "no-no" is a no-no), you need only consult Barzun. And
if you feel like being reminded of the essentials of interesting
travel writing, or of the art of conducting a provocative interview, or of the secret of why Red Smith is different from most
other sports writers, all you have to do is browse through
Zinsser.

And yet I wonder if these books are really going to help
the people to whom their messages are primarily directed—
the students who go on turning out comma splices after being

told a dozen times what constitutes an elementary sentence, or the stock-market analysts who write of "upside gravity" even though a moment's sober reflection would expose the absurdity of such a notion. Why is it that Americans keep fouling the atmosphere with their verbiage, even when the academic woods are filled with instructors like Mr. Barzun and Mr. Zinsser and every branch of the English curriculum bears leaves of Fowler's *Usage* and White's *Elements*? (As a matter of fact, how come after carefully reading these two books I myself suddenly felt as if I couldn't rub two coherent sentences together?)

I know, I know. It's laziness and lack of discipline that account for the impurities of our prose, and more recently— if a recent *Newsweek* cover story has it right—it's a mindlessness induced by watching television and listening to 1960's liberals (illiberals?) who said that any way you felt like saying it was right. Still, I wonder if it isn't also partly the tone of our instructors that's at fault—a tone that is typified by the rhetoric of *Simple & Direct* and *On Writing Well*.

Clutter and fuzziness

They exhort us, do Messrs. Barzun and Zinsser. They tell us to banish the clutter from our prose, to cease thinking so fuzzily, to sensitize ourselves to the meaning of language, and to sanitize the prose we are perpetrating. Improve yourself, they tell us—which means that there is something very wrong with us. And it doesn't take too many steps, especially reading Mr. Barzun, to figure out that what's wrong is that we're lazy, ignorant, inattentive, badly read, poorly bred and dumb.

Yes, I know that these instructors don't mean us to understand everything all at once. I know that these books are meant to be consulted and reconsulted as one's writing progresses from subliteracy to coherence. Still, even I, who should know better, began these books by feeling defensive. (I found myself jumping at Mr. Zinsser for writing "If I may belabor the metaphor of carpentry . . . ," when he ought to have written "labor"; I chortled triumphantly at the ambiguity in Mr. Barzun's instruction to "Lead up to the object without a break"; and I wondered incredulously how he could offer us as an example of good diction a sentence of Eric Hoffer's that begins, "This lack of worship goes hand in hand with the fact that in normal times. . . .") And by the end I had thought so much about the elements of good writing that I felt unable to write.

And so I wonder what students and other struggling writers must feel when we exhort them with the message that something is terribly wrong with them. Apparently they don't feel like writing better. Perhaps what we ought to be doing instead is searching for deeper causes to explain inarticulateness—causes such as the ones George Orwell was after when he wrote *Politics and the English Language*, or chromosomes that have intelligence, or the lack of it, attached to them. As for books like *Simple & Direct*, and *On Writing Well*—they are really meant for people who already know how to write.

Doris Grumbach is a Senior Editor of *Saturday Review*, for which she writes a regular book review column called "Fine Print." She was formerly literary editor of *The New Republic*, writes a monthly column for *The New York Times Book Review*, and reviews for various magazines and newspapers. She is Professor of American Literature at American University. Some of the material in this chapter first appeared in *Washington Review of the Arts*.

3

A Review of the Craft of Reviewing

An interview with Doris Grumbach

Q. *Is it important for a reviewer to describe a book in objective terms so the reader can make an independent judgment of it?*

A. I think one has to deal with the book fully: what it is, what it contains, what the author is trying to do, not what the reviewer thinks he *should* be doing, not what the reviewer has decided ought to be in the book, but what *is* there. It is the reviewer's job to make comparisons to other books in the same genre, to set it among other similar cultural manifestations, in other words, to give the reader every kind of objective help possible to make his own judgment. I don't think that reviews that barely touch upon the contents are fair or helpful. If that is what you mean by "objective," yes, there should be that content. To a great extent, many critics don't trouble to do this. In addition, it's the responsible reviewer's job to read at least some of the *oeuvre* of the writer, not just the book at hand, but perhaps the five or six other works that precede it. This is why it is so difficult and financially unrewarding to be a reviewer.

Q. *Should the reviewer make "value judgments" or simply try to inspire curiosity and awareness?*
A. In the very act of choosing a book to review (or agreeing to review it), one makes a value judgment. Criticism without value judgments is mere cataloguing, a kind of handy list-making which has no possible value for the reader. What one needs to do as a professional reviewer is to establish one's credentials as a thoughtful, responsible person who considers a book as carefully as he can and is educated to do, and then provides the reader with a judgment he hopes is right. If you stay in the business long enough, readers begin to know who and what you are as a reviewer. They will either respect what you have recommended to them or not, whichever way it goes. There are people who go to the theater to see precisely the plays that a particular critic doesn't like— a negative manner of choosing: "If he doesn't like it, I will." In book reviewing, there are people who say, "Well, if she likes it, I will read it." But even if I wished to, I'm certain it's impossible to eliminate value judgments. There is no such thing as the completely objective reviewer. So it is a great responsibility to take care to make your judgments valid, fair and responsible.

Q. *Do you find that you do a better review of a book when you like it or when you don't like it? Are the best reviewers lovers or haters?*
A. I used to enjoy writing negative reviews, because it allowed me to indulge my prose style, and I loved that. But since the time I was a book editor, and now as a reviewer,

I'm aware of the tragic lack of space for the notice of good books. Now I think it is a shame to waste space on a negative review, unless the book has an enormous reputation which you feel is overblown and you would like to deflate it. Or unless it's an enormous best seller, and you think it's a terrible book on which people ought not to waste their money. But to waste space and time on a poor book, which would be better consigned to oblivion without further notice, seems to me foolish.

I am fortunate, now, to be able to choose the books I review. I read galleys and write to the places I review for and say, "I have found a book I want to review." My motive in this is always that I like the book, and want to spend my time working on it.

Q. *Do you ever attack a book you don't like, by writing a harsh review?*
A. I have done such reviews. A couple of years ago I did a destructive piece on Anaïs Nin, whose reputation seems to me to be completely out of proportion to the essential silliness of her product. I've taken books that I think were utterly foolish and said so. But my preference really is not to do this, but to find relatively unknown writers and try to make the public aware of their excellence.

This year I have reviewed the novels of two such writers: William Kennedy and Mary Gordon. Other people have taken Gordon (*Final Payments*) up, too. I am pleased at that. Kennedy is still looking for his public. I hope my long review of *Billy Phelan's Last Game*, his new book and third novel, will stir some interest. If you take reviewing seriously you develop a kind of apostolic feeling for your work. You find yourself proclaiming your discoveries as if you had been entrusted with a gospel to preach.

Q. *How authoritative should a reviewer be in a review?*
A. As authoritative as I can make it. I bring to bear all the periphery of scholarship; I try to document my assertions, to illustrate what I claim with examples from the book. I think that's very important in reviews, to provide solid examples from the book if you are talking about style. I often do this, because how the book is written is one of the things I care about. If I think a book is well written, I try to quote some of its prose. And of course, I do this if I think it is not. I think a wishy-washy review is useless. A review that's a book report is a waste of space. Certainly, much ego goes into this business. You feel that your judgment is valuable and right. But it could be wrong, and many times I have been wrong. But I project my views with the same sense of rectitude, the same horrifying sureness, as if they were infallible.

Q. *Do you prefer a review that is fair, honest, and dull, to one that is interesting but idiosyncratic? In other words, should the review be a literary production on its own?*
A. It is, for me, the greatest temptation in the world to be so charming, so enchantingly delightful in a review that the reader will be taken with me and my style in the review and forget the book. When I find myself doing that, I throw it out and start again. Such self-indulgence is unfair to the author of the book you are considering, and fraudulent for the reader. You ought, I think, to be transparent as you write, so that nothing in your style, or your manner of reviewing, will call attention to your presence in the review. That's the ideal; I'm not sure I always achieve it, and I know many other reviewers who suffer from the same temptation.

Q. *How do you deal with the subject of the author's in-*

tention? Is it ever acceptable for a reviewer to criticize the intent or the point of view of an author of a book?

A. In reviewing both fiction and nonfiction, I try to understand as much of the writer's intent as I can, and to accept it. I try to blot out, if I can—to purify, in almost a spiritual sense, my prejudgments of how it should have been handled, how it should have been done. I try to enter into the book as a thing in itself, to see how that particular thing the author set himself to do works. It's especially hard to do in reviewing nonfiction, because there you are looking for excellence of scholarship. But I try, or at least that's my intention.

In fiction, it is always my intention. In *The Art of Fiction*, Henry James says that fiction is a tower with a thousand windows. At every window stands a writer. Obviously, the expressed vision is going to be different from every window. The critic cannot make a judgment about where the writer's eyes should have been located or should look or what they should have seen. It's a very thorny problem, what one brings as expectation to a book. I think the less you expect, the better you are at judging it.

I think you need to begin every book of fiction you intend to review in a state of what can only be described as innocence. Purity is another possible word; you want to be emptied of your preferences, your prejudices, your past. Then the magic of a book (if it has the magic you are always waiting for) will work on you. If I weren't afraid of using such theological language I would say the reviewer dealing with a book in this untainted way is in a state of grace. Only a happy relationship can come in the resultant review. John Updike, in the introduction to his excellent volume of criticism, *Picked-up Pieces*, says: "The communion between a reviewer and his public is based upon the presumption of certain possible joys of reading, and all our discriminations should curve toward that end."

Q. *What kind of general preparation—not expectation— should you have or bring to the reviewing of a book?*
A. Reading, in general, and as much as possible. I find that I still read about two books a day. A lot of it goes into that vast compost heap that is my subconscious, and out of which I hope I will make better judgments than those I would make if I had not read or listened or heard as much as I have. I'm not saying that I've reached any great plateau of wisdom, but the richer the compost heap the better and more valuable my opinion of a book may be.

Q. *How do you measure the audience you reach? Is it possible to assume that your readers have a common body of knowledge so that you can refer to it and expect most of them to recognize and understand your references?*
A. That depends a great deal on where the reviews are appearing. If you're doing a review for a literary review or quarterly, you can assume that most of your references will be understood by the readers. Since I do, to some extent, make my living as a writer, however, I write primarily for newspapers and magazines. There I cannot make the assumption of a common culture to which one can refer in reviews. I try, therefore, as much as possible to make my references informative and not simply provocative, so that the reader will not feel excluded from a large area of learning he knows nothing about. I don't think the point of a review is to demonstrate the learning of the reviewer to an ignorant audience. If I do make references that might be unfamiliar to the general reader, I try to explain them so that the reader might say, "Aha, that's something I ought to look up." The field of

reference for reviewers in the national press has narrowed to popular culture. If you refer to Kojak, you're safe, but if you refer to a story by Kate Chopin, you're not. You can't be pedantic, unless you're given the space, and you take the trouble, to explain your pedantry.

What I try to do is to say to myself, "I like this book enormously, I'm going to try to interest as many people as I can in it." Occasionally I trim a little, because too much scholarship and pedantry lose the reader. The purpose of the review is to hold the reader long enough to interest him in the book.

Q. *Do you believe that too many books are being published?*
A. I've heard this said many times. The argument is that if fewer books were published, there would be a reduction in costs for the publisher and the book buyer, and consequently better books would be published, noticed and flourish. Many times, faced with an avalanche of books to be sorted out in order to select books to be reviewed, I found myself sharing that view. But it was only temporary. Always I come back to the painful truth that the more books published, the more chance for the exceptional, the avant-garde, to see the light of print. Under a cutback in titles, what would go? Those first novels and books of poetry that are chancy. Faced with necessary cuts in their budgets, publishers naturally tend to eliminate the unprofitable and concentrate on the guaranteed money-makers. The long shots will never get to run.

Q. *How do you assess the overall quality of the books that are published?*
A. I used to think that most of what is published is junk, but after my two years as a literary editor (during which time I read about 450 books and assigned about 500 others

for review), I found that almost everything published has some value to someone. About one quarter of what one sees in print is of some little value, another quarter is good or important or both, another twenty-five percent is both valuable and likely to endure. The last quarter is junk, of little value to anyone but the author. One looks at it and can only think of the trees that were slaughtered to give it life. If one could be sure that this valueless junk would be cut in a reduction of titles—well, that would be fine.

Q. *Are there some publishing houses whose books tend more often than not to fall into the quarter that is "good or important," or even "valuable and likely to endure"?*
A. Of course. I've acquired a genuine respect for most of the products of a few intelligent commercial publishers. Everyone who reads knows who they are and trusts their lists. In addition, I've formed an admiring acquaintance with the work of university and some small presses, both of which often are worth more review space than they now receive. The voices of silence that used to greet their books are explainable in two ways: (1) many book editors underestimated their readers, and (2) there was a tendency to overlook the small presses and university houses, most of which are located west of the Hudson, north of the Spuyten Duyvil Creek, and south of the Verrazano Bridge.

Q. *As a literary editor, how did you deal with the problem of choosing the right reviewer for a particular book? How do you make a good "match"?*
A. Sometimes individuals ask to review certain books. Generally, it is up to the editor to find the right person to review a book. I've noted three dangerous categories of persons who ask to review books: friends of the writer, enemies of the

writer, and the academic who has just completed his thesis on the writer and now wants an opportunity to display his erudition. The friend may spoil the review with unwarranted praise, the enemy with self-serving destructive spume, and the well-meaning scholar may drown it in academic ambiguities and critical jargon.

In certain special areas, it was often hard to know just where to turn. For example, take the subject of slavery. There are five or six first-rate people writing in the area of slavery. There is a deep fissure in their views. How do you deal with the subject fairly without the obvious ploy of running two reviews—one pro and one con—a device which totally confuses the reader? You have to take a chance and hope that the reviewer will be honest in his bias. I respect the reviewer who shares his bias with the reader. Then the reader is in a position to say, "Well, this is a good review, because I understand where the reviewer stands," or, "This is not a reviewer whose judgment I can accept, because I suspect it is based on a strong bias."

Q. *Do readers really care, generally, who writes a review? Do "name" reviewers sell books?*
A. My notion is that most readers are, in the main, indifferent to the name of the reviewer. They will read the review only if the reviewer has caught their interest, has forced them to look hard at what he is saying about the book. Only the editor, the publisher of the book, and perhaps the author, worry about who the reviewer is.

Q. *Where are the best reviewers to be found?*
A. There is no way of generalizing about this. There are poor academic reviewers and equally poor literary journalists. Academic persons will often (gladly) review for nothing, to

see their names in print, or to add to their list of publications for college rank and tenure committees. There are, of course, academic reviewers who write in order to have a wider audience for their views than the scholarly journals afford. There are a few excellent academic reviewers who write for none of these reasons, who often accomplish a miracle of kindness toward their intellectual opponents and make good reading at the same time, especially if they write clear, unjargoned prose.

I think the persons I respect most, whose judgments I trust most among reviewers, are the professionals, people like Barbara Bannon at *Publishers Weekly*, Jonathan Yardley in Miami, and Robert Kirsch in Los Angeles, the people on the *Times Book Review*, John Leonard and Richard Locke, Wilfred Sheed, now at the Book-of-the-Month Club, and others like them, who make a career of criticism, who read constantly, judge regularly, and acquire an eye and an ear for interesting writing which no one who works at it sporadically can do.

A wise editor will search for new young reviewers to develop and support. In this way, he avoids the predictable response of the well-known, established reviewers. It is the unexpected, fresh reaction that is most rewarding to the reader.

Q. *What are some of the rewards of book reviewing?*
A. Above all the pitfalls and possible pratfalls are the towering peaks of pleasure. I've found it rewarding to come upon a book that I have had no advance warning about, to feel pure delight at its accomplishments, and to proclaim my delight in print. There is an even keener pleasure in discovering a book that no one else seems to have noticed at all, in persisting in liking it despite its neglect by reviewers and

readers, and then coming upon a reader who has been persuaded by your enthusiasm. One such book for me was E. F. Schumacher's *Small Is Beautiful*. I found it quite by accident and reviewed it. I'm proud of the small part I played with that review in helping to make it a continuing best seller, reprinted year after year, hundreds of thousands of copies of it, even going into hardback after years in paper. This is what the critical profession is all about: Excited discovery, the communication of it, some outside response to one's enthusiasm, "the word" passed from one mind to another.

B. A. BERGMAN, formerly book editor of *The Philadelphia Bulletin,* is now a book columnist for that paper. He served previously as a managing editor of *The New Yorker,* feature editor of *The Philadelphia Record,* and editor of *The Philadelphia Bulletin Sunday Magazine.*

4 | Do's and Don'ts of Book Reviewing

by B. A. BERGMAN

IF YOU want to be a book reviewer there are a number of don'ts that you must avoid. Assuming that you write simple, clear English (if you don't, better give up the idea), don't show off your erudition with smart-aleck exotica. Your job is to measure the worth of a book, not to demonstrate the variety of your vocabulary.

What does a reader want to know about a book? He wants to know the basics, of course: the title, author, number of pages, price and the publisher. Some publishers are known for the excellence of their product, and then there are some publishers who deal in junk. You can save time by knowing who they are.

A reader is not interested in your thoughts about politics or philosophy or whatever the subject of the book might be. How often have you noticed a review of a book that interested you, but then you had to fight through columns of the critic's own opinions before he got to the subject of the book? The critic enjoys showing off, but the frustrated reader who might have been interested in the book goes on to something else.

And then there's the critic who tells you how he would have written the book. That's not what the reader wants to know. Readers are interested in how the author wrote it.

I like short reviews. The Book Page in *The Bulletin* is limited to a page, so reviews must out of necessity be short. Our longest reviews are seldom over 400 words, our shortest often less than 100 words. Surprising what you can say about a book in 100 words. For good examples of short reviews which give you the evaluation you are seeking, there are *The New Yorker* reviews which follow the main (and occasionally too long) lead review. *Publishers Weekly*, the magazine of the publishing industry, runs about 100 reviews a week. They are short and very much to the point. Barbara Bannon, executive editor of the magazine, oversees the work of dozens of anonymous skilled reviewers. They are evaluating books for the bookseller and they do it beautifully. Ms. Bannon is probably the most influential critic in America. Praise from *PW* stimulates sales. Their track record is unusually high. I recommend to the neophyte reviewer that he study *Publishers Weekly* and the short reviews in *The New Yorker*.

Don't try to emulate Dorothy Parker, who could devastate a book in one sentence. There was only one Dorothy Parker. She was usually giving her opinion of a book or author she couldn't stand and cut him down quickly. A. A. Milne was one of her targets. About *The House at Pooh Corner*, Milne at his sentimental heights, "Constant Reader" (her critical byline) said simply: "Tonstant weader fwoed up." Hardly a fair judgment, but a good opinion of the book for those who felt about Milne as Miss Parker did. But it's hardly an example of a good book review, unless you have the Parker skill and a Milnesque target.

Don't let best-seller lists influence you. A best seller does not indicate the worth of a book, simply that more people are buying it, often for reasons not related to literary excellence. And best sellers are often phony. David Shaw, the investigative reporter of *The Los Angeles Times* assigned to the media, blasted best-seller lists in a well-documented article. He even included his own newspaper, which gulped but took it courageously. He quoted me as stating that best-seller lists were often dishonest, that it was easy to place any book on the best-seller list if you worked at it. One way is for an author or a publisher to buy a sufficient number of books to have the stores report it. Movie companies also do it, for it's important, they feel, if an advertisement shouts in 48-point type that *The Cry of the Abandoned* was on the best-seller lists for weeks. One of the glaring examples of making a book a best seller for its appeal to the movie customers was Erich Segal's *Love Story*. It was originally written as a scenario. Then when Paramount decided that it should first be a novel, Segal easily added some "she saids" and "he saids" to the tightly-written script. Paramount then proceeded, as it was reported in the trade, to spend $25,000 on the book in key bookstores. It became a best seller immediately. Ironically, the book didn't require the Paramount money to climb ahead, for it caught on immediately. (P.S. I liked it.)

Many reviews mean little, for they are written by friends of the author, dripping glowing adjectives about the book's merits. Conversely, if the critic dislikes an author, he may pan a book which deserves praise. So if you want to be a critic, don't attempt to review books of friends or enemies. Take a book of an author personally unknown to you and give your candid judgment.

Well, what makes a good review? Remember you are writing for an audience that reads and may even want to purchase a book or two. Or at least to borrow it from a friend, an abominable practice. I never lend my books, but if a friend asks for one I buy it for him.

First of all, describe briefly what the book is about. Tell something about the author, his previous works, or tell if it's a first novel. Readers like to know the background of an author especially to note whether he's writing on a subject he's familiar with. John Updike, we know, is an expert on Connecticut suburban adultery; Norman Mailer is an expert on everything journalistic and he did write one of the great novels of World War II—*The Naked and the Dead.*

The size of a book is important. James Michener writes long, long books but knows how to tell a story so the length does not affect their appeal. James M. Cain, who broke into overnight fame with his first novel, *The Postman Always Rings Twice,* writes tighter than any writer I have ever read. He rewrites and rewrites. Try to find an unnecessary word in any of his books. Alfred Knopf, who published *The Postman,* insisted that it was too short, but every time he returned it for Cain to increase its length, Cain always shortened it.

The reader should also know something about the critic's background to determine whether he has sufficient knowledge of the subject. Usually the blurb describing the critic at the end of the review should suffice. A professor of poetry, say, like Daniel Hoffman at the University of Pennsylvania, will give a book of poetry a sound and honest review. For books on national politics, espcially about the President, the reviewer should be familiar with the Washington scene. Robert Roth, a veteran Washington correspondent and a past presi-

dent of the prestigious Gridiron Club, is excellent on such
books. He reviews them brilliantly for the *Bulletin* in concise,
simple language.

One of the features of the *Bulletin* Book Page is the short
review under 100 words. A skillful writer can tell all the
reader needs to know about a book in 100 words or so.
(The reviewer, incidentally, should receive equal payment
with the author of a 400-word review. That's the policy followed by the *Bulletin*, for it's often more difficult to write
an intelligent 100-word review than it is to cover a book in
400.) Rose DeWolf, a star *Bulletin* columnist, is adept at
this. Here is a typical DeWolf "short":

> In *The Fan* by Bob Randall (Random House, $7.95), we
> get to know aging Broadway star Sally Ross through the
> letters she writes and the letters written to her. There is a
> certain kick to reading other people's mail—even when the
> letters are fictional.
>
> Anway, we get to like Sally and we start to worry as the
> letters from one fan turn from admiring to possessive to
> hateful. We know he's nuts. We fear for Sally's life. The
> tension builds. The end is a real shocker. Nifty.
>
> —Rose DeWolf

Reprinted from the Sunday Book Page of *The Philadelphia Bulletin*.
Copyright © 1977, The Bulletin Company.

Do you need to know any more about *The Fan* than Rose
DeWolf tells in 87 words? Obviously, many books can be
disposed of in 100 words, though not the giants—the reader
is entitled to a more comprehensive estimate of them.

John Ehrlichman's novel, *The Company*, was highly praised
in many longish reviews. Did any critic you may have read
tell it more effectively than Robert Fuoss in the *Bulletin?*
Fuoss, whose review follows, was the last editor of the old

Saturday Evening Post and has a passion for clear writing that was a feature of the *Post*. His review tells everything about *The Company* that you should know to pass judgment on it. It tells fully who Ehrlichman was, his writing skill, and enough of the plot to entice you to read it. Fuoss also predicted that Ehrlichman would make a lot of money from it. He did. Here is the Fuoss review:

The Company, by John Erlichman
Simon & Schuster   313 pp. $8.95
by Robert Fuoss

John Ehrlichman's first novel is destined to be a major topic of political gossip this Presidential summer, and I regret to report may well earn the big dollar for this man the nation has so little reason to reward.

Ehrlichman was Nixon's deputy for domestic affairs. He was found guilty of conspiracy, obstruction of justice and perjury in the Watergate trial. Free on appeal, he has used the interval to turn out *The Company*—a far better novel than he could have been expected to produce. Ehrlichman, in fact, has a superb eye for detail, and he writes with a clinical savagery that is made to order for his chilling tale of political intrigue.

The Company, otherwise known as the CIA, is the primary setting for Ehrlichman's novel. Three Presidents figure in the story. The first (Kennedy?) orders the CIA's director to assassinate a Dominican revolutionary. The second (Johnson?) protects the director from reprisal. The third (Nixon?) tries to use the assassination for his own political ends—with results that may remind you of Watergate itself.

What gives *The Company* its special savor, however, is Ehrlichman's intimate experience at the seat of power. Never before, to my knowledge, has Presidential privacy been so thoroughly penetrated—nor the artfulness of command so totally exposed.

It is this sense of ruthless authenticity that will stimulate readers to wonder whether the characters are, in truth, thinly-disguised real people. Is "Flaherty" Haldeman? Is "Tessler" Kissinger? Is Ehrlichman telling it like it was, girls and all, or is he using a fictional cover to pay off some old scores?

Unhappily, you can't join this juicy guessing game without lining Ehrlichman's pockets in the process. Oh, well! Considering his probable future, he may find it very hard to enjoy the money.

Raymond C. Brecht is a star rewrite man of the *Bulletin*. He appears frequently on its Book Page, for Brecht tackles a book as he does an intricate news story. His review of *Wild Pitch*, by A. B. Guthrie, Jr., appears here. Brecht doesn't like to review books that he doesn't care for. He cares for Guthrie, and his review of *Wild Pitch* tells everything that you should know about the book, plus Guthrie's background. If you can read this review and not rush to secure the book, I'll be surprised. Rewrite men as knowledgeable as Brecht, with his wide journalistic experience, make superb critics. Perhaps you need a stint as a rewrite man before tackling book reviews.

Wild Pitch, by A. B. Guthrie, Jr.
Houghton Mifflin   224 pp. $5.95
by Raymond C. Brecht

Imagine the easy rhythms of a small western town. Plain people. Names like Loose Lip Lancaster and Taller-Ass McNair. An old lady who sings hymns on her way to the post office. A sheriff with horse sense. Suddenly, a sniper kills a man at a picnic, then another at his mailbox, at midnight.

That's the texture of *Wild Pitch,* the new novel by A. B.

Guthrie, Jr. He's the Montana-raised newspaper editor (in Lexington, Ky.) who wrote *The Way West* (Pulitzer Prize, 1952), *The Big Sky* and others.

This book is a dazzling change of pace. It's not about the sweep of western wind and sky, although there are the familiar touches, or about galloping horses and thundering herds. It's as homey as the Commercial Cafe, which serves grub for the guests in the local jail.

It's told in an earthy idiom that fits the people like their working clothes. It tells with engaging simplicity how Chick Charleston, the young sheriff who rarely wears a gun, figures out the sniper shootings, and the why of them.

Jason Beard, 17-year-old pitcher for the local baseball team and an unofficial Watson to the sheriff, is on the scene every step of the neighborly investigation. Jason tells the story in a style as striking as the sun on a western afternoon, sharp as the shadows in Mrs. Jenkins' chicken yard.

Western backdrop

The western backdrop is in the Guthrie manner. The town is Midbury (pop. 1,500) and there are places with names like Bear Paw. There's the scent of pine. Mountains rise gaunt and blue against a bluer sky. It seems an unlikely setting for murder and suspense. But amateur finger-printing and country sense keep you alive and guessing until Jason throws his fast ball at exactly the right time.

Jason, for all his youth, has the eyes and ears of A. B. Guthrie. He seems born to spin a lighthearted western mystery, as the book is billed. Guthrie has had a fine romp.

This book is no trifle, happily written, as one might think, between weightier endeavors. It's a piece of artistry.

I haven't emphasized sufficiently the importance of clear, simple writing. Study *The Elements of Style*, by E. B. White and his Cornell English teacher, William Strunk, Jr. And after you have absorbed the stern injunctions of White and Strunk, I also recommend that you read E. B. White's essays. There's no more outstanding stylist in the land. There are other books on good writing, for suddenly we have discovered that we don't write simply enough to communicate with each other.

H. L. Mencken was a great reviewer, but don't try to ape his style. No one can successfully. Mencken was either enthusiastically for a writer or just as enthusiastically against. I wouldn't recommend his criticisms as guides, but for sheer entertainment and lusty writing no one has ever excelled him.

What's the best training for book reviewing? Most good critics were originally newspaper reporters. I'm not talking about reviewers who write scholarly dissertations, but about the gentry who write for the popular magazines and the daily press. As good reporters, they appreciate the value of clarity and are careful to write brief reviews, not the long pieces in the *Times Book Review*. I am not criticizing *The Times*; it is the world's greatest newspaper and considers itself the newspaper of record. Hence, it must tell all that goes into the record.

Are you familiar with the outstanding writers of today and yesterday? You'd better be if you want to be a critic of sound judgment.

If you want to make a career out of book reviewing, I hope you have other sources of income. Not many publications have full-time reviewers; in fact few newspapers, alas, pay much attention to books. And those that do usually farm out books to staffers for a small fee or no fee at all. The free lancer usually receives meager payment. Some newspapers "generously" let the reviewer keep the book as his payment. There's little market for the free-lance critic in the daily press. For if the newspaper wants to run some book reviews, it can use AP or UPI services, which include book reviews.

Book reviewing is usually a moonlighting occupation that fits in well with your life if you're in any part of the communications business or a teacher in subjects that are covered by books. There are a few lawyers who can write well, and they are excellent reviewers of books about some phase of the law.

If I haven't discouraged you and if you've done your homework, my blessings.

Lynne Sharon Schwartz is a free-lance fiction writer and reviewer. Her work has appeared in *Redbook, Transatlantic Review, Ms., The Saturday Review,* and many other periodicals.

5

The Making of a Reviewer

by Lynne Sharon Schwartz

I like to think of a book as a strange new geological treasure, a rock never before handled. The delighted discoverer's first, most natural response is, What have we here? I hold the rock in the palm of my hand to examine it: what are its colors, its contours, its special beauty (or ugliness)? Is it like others I've seen, enough like them, even, to fit into a generic category? Is it more or less beautiful than those of its kind? Or is it, though it bears a surface family resemblance, distinguished by intriguing, individual markings?

The "what have we here" approach will yield a reviewer fruitful results. Every book deserves this careful attention; every one is unique—though some uniquely bad—and demands to be judged for its intrinsic, living qualities. The opposite approach might be labeled "negative criticism." The negative critic appraises a book on the basis of what it has failed to accomplish, with these failings usually derived from the critic's own notion of how he or she would have handled the subject. Not only unfair but misleading, too. For a critic's job is to leave aside his own musings and try temporarily to share the author's view. What has the author set out to do? is the crucial question.

Now, it is far easier to be explicit about the goals of nonfiction than of fiction. When I recently reviewed a biography of Alice B. Toklas, it was not difficult to decide whether or not the book gave an accurate, coherent, inclusive account of Toklas' life. (The larger question of how well it does so is another matter.) Again, in *Literary Women*, Ellen Moers set out to prove a specific point about 19th and 20th century women writers. I became convinced that she had amply done that, and said so in my review. But it is far harder to be unequivocal about fiction, since fiction at its best does not set out to prove or to do anything. To say that *Anna Karenina* "shows" what happens to an upper class 19th-century Russian woman who commits adultery would be literary blasphemy. Fiction is the working out of an inner vision; it is impossible to "judge" anyone's vision, and quite a delicate matter to evaluate its metamorphosis into words.

Still, the thing has to be done. Books must be brought to the attention of the public, and reviewers must eat and pay rent. So we might glance at some of the more touchy problems of how it is to be done. First, though, a cautionary word: if you believe that what a specific author has set out to do is not worth doing, better to pass up that book and choose another. The book deserves a fighting chance, and you as critic deserve a more worthwhile application of your talents. When you find yourself in that fascinating gray area, however, where criticism needs to focus on the gap between worthy aims and slightly less worthy achievements, take a deep breath and plunge in. Those will be the hardest reviews to write but the most satisfying to look back on.

A paid reviewer has certain obligations to an audience

which sound exceedingly obvious yet are too often ignored. First, to tell the reader what the book is: to return to the rock analogy, describe its size, shape, color, texture and distinctive marks. Second, to assess the author's intentions and say to what degree they've been met. That means—and here is what frightens many new reviewers—a personal judgment. In book reviewing, as in so much else, there is no way out of accountability for one's views. Certainly, don't review a book until you have the courage and authority to state your convictions honestly. But once you do, don't shrink from the truth: it is, after all, what the editor hired you for.

Here again, a caution on the opposite side may be in order. A few columns in a magazine do confer a certain power, glamorous at first. It is best not to use this power for the airing of resentment or grievances. In my own case, for example, I would never request for review the novels of a particular best-selling author, because I know I could barely control myself from lacerating her work in print. Though the work might well deserve it, my motives could hardly be termed pure!

Next, a reviewer needs to say specifically what is in the book; if nonfiction, the premises on which it is based and the conclusions it reaches, the major issues and points raised along the way, the extent and thoroughness with which they are covered. If it is fiction, the themes, the areas and vicissitudes of life the author is preoccupied with. Plot summaries, as we all remember from school, should be minimal. But a dash of the reporter's standard questions—where, what, when, how, and why—will prove helpful. Above all, a discussion of the nature and interaction of the characters as they grow from the novel's inception through its development and close, is essential.

Last, and possibly most important, is an evaluation of

style. Books, our fact-oriented age tends to forget, are made of words, in the best instances deftly laced together to create a surface that mirrors or complements its subject. Everyone, in the privacy of his brain, spins theories and fantasies. Only a writer labors to put the theories or fantasies into words. It is precisely for this labor with words, as much as for the quality of the content, that a book should be assessed. What is the flavor of the author's special idiom? Does the style aid or hinder the emergence of the themes? An even bigger question, does the use of words enhance or detract from the richness and capacity of our common inherited language?

There have been authors in whom the great disparity between style and content has distressed reviewers. Theodore Dreiser's early critics, for example, fairly unanimously agreed that his style was graceless and at times atrocious. Yet the potency of his social vision and the undeniable reality of his characters apparently redeemed him. But such a case is an anomaly. The contrary can happen too: in reviewing a first novel for *Ms. Magazine*, I said the author had wit, verve, a fine ear for dialogue and a remarkable aptness for metaphor, but the subject she had chosen was simply too narrow for her talents. I encouraged her to find something broader to write about (kindness, so long as it does not interfere with honesty, does no harm), and was rewarded by her writing to thank me for my "sensitive" review!

Since books are composed of words, ideally an astute, literate reviewer should be able to handle a book on any subject, and indeed some national magazines have tried assigning books to critics outside the field. Joyce Carol Oates did a fine review for *The New York Times Book Review* of Lewis Thomas's *Lives of a Cell*, a doctor's and biologist's penetrating look at life processes and cycles; her success was probably due less to an extensive knowledge of biology than to an appreciation of the book's lucid style and mellow, humanist outlook. Practically speaking, however, such a happy pairing is rare. I might be able to tell you whether a book on economics presents a cogent, well-expressed theory in terms of its own aims and limitations, but I could not evaluate its position in economic history, its relation to politics, international relations, and so on, for lack of knowledge. As a beginning reviewer, get to know as thoroughly as possible the field you choose to work in.

When I started reviewing, I felt competent to write about current fiction, since I had read it all my life, taken the college and graduate courses that presumably qualify one to make intelligent discriminations, taught literature, and was a fiction writer myself. Also, I had followed the growth of the feminist movement with sympathy and personal involvement and thought I particularly understood what women writers were saying (though I was not always a whole-hearted admirer of the aesthetic results). Typically, with my first reviews I was overprepared—not a bad thing to be, as it turned out. I made sure I was familiar with an author's earlier books so I could see the latest one in the context of a body of work. Naturally this meant more crammed reading and time spent in relation to money earned than was comfortable, but I felt I owed this to the author and my readers. I still do. (Anyone reading this is surely aware that reviewing is not one of life's more lucrative occupations.) Often, especially in brief reviews, hardly more than a sentence or two referring to the earlier works found its way into my final draft, yet I felt that my background knowledge improved the review and gave it a justified tone of authority.

In the case of an established and prolific writer such as Iris Murdoch, whose novel *A Word Child* I reviewed for *The Nation*, I would not have requested the book had I not

read and enjoyed most of her dozen or so earlier novels.
Another example is the first review I ever wrote, for *The
New Republic,* of the Italian author Natalia Ginzburg's
novel, *No Way.* Ginzburg has always been one of my
favorite writers, one I feel is unfortunately too little known
in the United States. In the review, a labor of love, I found
myself writing a general essay about her abiding themes and
past work, and setting the new novel in the framework of
these. Admittedly, I was trying to educate American readers.
Luckily, *The New Republic*'s Literary Editor at the time,
Doris Grumbach, welcomed personal initiative on the part
of reviewers.

I had trepidations for some time about reviewing nonfiction. What could I claim to know about real facts in the
real world? Nevertheless, intrigued by the advance publicity,
I asked to review Ellen Moers' *Literary Women* for *The
Nation.* Faced with the book's wealth of data, presented by
someone who had evidently read every word penned by a
woman over the past 200 years, I felt incompetent. Yet oddly
enough, as I read the book, not only did great forgotten
chunks of my early studies return to me, but I found whatever else I needed to know on its pages. In my review, besides
giving the usual information, I turned my attention partly
to the controversy the book had engendered by its considering women authors apart from men, a controversy on which
I had very definite and educated opinions.

Encouraged by that breaking of the nonfiction barrier, so
to speak, I requested of *Ms. Magazine* Ann Cornelisen's
Women of the Shadows, about the lives of Southern Italian
peasant women. Here I worried that my ignorance of agricul-
tural economy, of the difficulties of industrialization, and
such, would hamper me. However, I had read other books
on the region, and had lived in Italy and traveled through

the areas Cornelisen wrote about. I hoped that this firsthand knowledge would stand me in good stead, and I believe it did. I hasten to add, though, that I would hesitate to review a similar book on the lives of peasant women in Turkey or Morocco, places I know nothing about.

In brief, know your subject by study or by firsthand experience, or both. Then if, as occasionally will happen, you are given a book you feel overwhelmed by, stick to what you know and perceive, avoid grandiose generalities, and in the end, trust your instincts. Above all, don't attempt to sound authoritative when there is no basis for authority. I remember how pleased I was to be offered a book by *The Chicago Tribune Book World*, but how distressed on opening the desired package to find a novel of World War II, filled with details of military strategy, sabotage, fortifications, and the rest. I knew nothing personally about war, still less about military strategy, and besides, I had strong negative feelings about both. Nevertheless I turned to page one with a sense of duty. I found in the book itself all I needed to know about strategy, and found in addition, to my pleasant surprise, that like all good novels, *Kramer's War*, by Derek Robinson, was about human beings working out their complex, connected destinies in a situation of great stress. I was able not only to review it but to enjoy it as well. Needless to say, though, I avoided undue discussion of strategy, fortifications, or deployment of troops.

The above remarks apply once you have the book in hand, but a more pressing question for the novice reviewer is probably, How do you get the books assigned? Timing is of the essence. Since newspapers' Sunday sections are prepared weeks ahead and magazines often months ahead, you need to know what titles are coming out well in advance of publication date. *Publishers Weekly*, the invaluable trade magazine, lists forthcoming books, as does *Library Journal*. From their brief and pithy descriptions you can find which books are suitable for you.

Getting the first assignment is difficult, yet a newcomer's prospects are not totally bleak. It's best to try your local papers or weeklies first, even if it means working for no pay temporarily—certainly not advisable as a long-term habit, but worth the initial sacrifice. Send the editor a sample review, your best effort of course, with the names of several forthcoming books you'd like to try, and a few persuasive lines telling why you are especially qualified to review them. Don't be daunted if a first try fails. The erosion technique—wearing down a solid, recalcitrant object by a light, steady trickle—has been known to work. Once you have established yourself locally you might try larger markets, sending around tear sheets of previous work. By all means follow up any leads from friends or colleagues. When book review editors send out the word that they're looking for new writers, they usually mean it.

It's extremely important to be aware of the tastes, readership, slants, if any, space limitations, and general tone of the magazine you're writing for. The last quality may be hard to define but is easy enough to discern. Your chances of impressing *The National Review* with an iconoclastic critique of capitalism are about as great as of getting a laudatory review of *The Total Woman* into *The Village Voice*. In a realistic way, try to suit your review to the publication. If this requires too great a dislocation of your own values, better to try elsewhere. I have found it possible to write for varied periodicals without doing damage to my fundamental opinions about a book. When reviewing *Women of the Shadows* for *Ms.*, I stressed its feminist aspects more than I would have, say, for *The Nation*, where I might have dwelt more on the inequities inherent in the system of land tenure. Both themes were vital and important—the choice was a matter of emphasis, bearing in mind the concerns of prospective readers.

Once you are in the hard-earned position of writing fairly freely for a number of places (that is, once editors have come to trust you), you will find that magazines vary greatly in the way they handle review copy. Very few editors print every word as written. Some, like Emile Capouya, former Literary Editor of *The Nation,* make changes so small, subtle and apt that I, for one, never noticed them at first, only felt vaguely that my review was better than I thought. Others ask for extensive changes, either for the "good" motives of style and coherence, or the "bad" motives of space, and sometimes for both.

One of my most valuable—though trying—experiences has been doing short (250-word) reviews for *The Saturday Review.* Not until I tried several did I realize how much more arduous and time-consuming they were than the long sort, where one can leisurely spin out an argument. More than once, when I believed I couldn't cut another syllable without violating both the spirit of the book and my own integrity, *SR*'s Book Review Editor came up with a suggestion that not only solved her paste-up problems but made the review sharper and more direct. The moral, I suppose, is to be cooperative with editors, whose experience is usually vast and long. (Unless, of course, their requests involve distorting your opinions for extraneous reasons, which is unacceptable and happens, at least to my knowledge, thankfully seldom.)

It goes without saying that a reviewer should strive to become an accomplished writer, with all the skills that nebulous adjective implies. Though this may be beyond anyone's power to teach, one can learn to be competent, and the old incitement to constant practice does work. If you have a germ of writing talent, careful nurture will yield results. Certainly competition is stiff and editors will pick the best people they can get. But if they discover someone with a dash of originality, a capacity for felicitous use of language, and a strong sense of organization, they will generally work with that person until the aptitudes can flourish independently. They also, incidentally, will be grateful for a readable, correctly spelled and punctuated manuscript, submitted on time.

Now, suppose you have won the coveted assignment and have the book in hand. How to proceed? The reading is often the hardest part of the job, very different from reading for pleasure, where you can enjoy as you choose, or if there is no pleasure, simply close the book. One reads with the unsettling sense of needing to remember everything, much like studying for an exam. I can offer only suggestions based on personal habit, and doubtless each reviewer will have his or her own idiosyncratic techniques. One thing you unquestionably owe the book and your audience, though, is a thorough reading. Authors frequently complain that their critics seem not to have read the book, or to have read some other book. There is no way of telling whether this is true, but at least new reviewers can avoid the imputation.

I usually read a book twice, once slowly with great concentration, occasionally marking passages along the way, and the second time quickly, to get a sense of overall shape, flow, and pattern. The reading is invariably accompanied by familiar conflicts which one learns to take in stride. If I am enjoying the book too much, I worry about losing objectivity, not paying enough attention to how the author achieves his or her effects and simply luxuriating in those effects. On the other hand, if I dislike the book, I make enormous efforts not to become resentful of my task and thus dislike it more than it may warrant. I try to look for good points that any one of my innumerable small prejudices may prevent me from noticing. In either case it is hardly relaxing.

To take or not to take notes is another dubious question. Marking luminous or striking passages, or simply noting their page numbers, is not too distracting—one learns to read with pen in hand—but stopping for real notes fragments the experience of reading. Note-taking during the second reading is more effective. After the two readings I write down my general impressions with illustrations from the book, and organize them under several inclusive headings, which gives me a loose outline. I then proceed with the best intentions of working from this outline, but habitually write the piece straight on, barely glancing at the notes until later, to see that I've covered everything and to locate appropriate examples. It might be suspected that the extra reading, note-taking and outlining are unnecessary effort. Yet in the end it seems that the intense preparation is somehow needed for the rather swift, "thoughtless" writing process. Also, the outline exists as security in case I run dry halfway through. I don't presume that this method of total immersion, a valiant semblance of scholarly organization, and then an abandoned dash to the finish line can work for anyone else. I do offer it to demonstrate the devious, cumbersome and perhaps funny, mysterious ways that reviews get written.

Next come the patient correcting, revising, cutting and moving of parts, drudgery to be sure, but performed with the immense relief of knowing that the thing *exists*, in need only of tinkering. Always, when the review is typed in final form and on its way to the mailbox, I get wild flashes of insight informing me my work is all wrong: I should have kept in what I cut out and cut out what I kept in. These hand-on-the-mailbox insights must be totally disregarded. They are an inevitable part of the writing process that can be counteracted with a brisk walk in the park or a candy bar. (It may help to keep the finished review for a few days to give it a last check before mailing.)

There are, in addition, a few outside impediments to straight thinking that a novice reviewer should be aware of. One is an author's reputation. Depending on the murky depths of a reviewer's secret nature, he or she may be tempted to encourage or to attack new writers (regardless of the merit of the work), or to sustain or prick the balloon of reputation of well-known writers (also regardless of merit). To these temptations, the adage "Know thyself" is the best antidote, followed by the admonition, "Guard against thyself or don't review the book at all." Reviewing books by friends or acquaintances—a common if doubtful practice—requires similar restraint or total abstinence.

Other reviews and publishers' blurbs are powerful obstacles as well. But while the first can be summarily dealt with (never read them till your own review is safely in the mail), advertising, jacket copy, or those ingratiating notes from the publicity staff telling how wonderful the book is, are less easy to avoid. It is wise to recognize at the outset that what publicity people say should be regarded as a skillful pass in a complex ball game. The serious danger enters if the un-initiated reviewer's expectations are raised. "Smith's new novel relentlessly plumbs the depths of A, with brilliant insights into B, so that his style is reminiscent of C and D, though paradoxically echoing the uniqueness of E." Smith's book may in fact be a fine one, but a neophyte reviewer diligently in search of those letters of the alphabet is sure to be disappointed, as well as blinded to the book's true worth.

The final questions that keep reviewers tossing in bed at night are, Have I praised a book that everyone will see immediately is idiotic? and Have I missed (panned) a masterpiece? The first is more easily dispensed with. It is unlikely that a competent reviewer, after years of reading, will fail to spot awful work. Moreover, it is probably more honorable to err on the side of generosity. But not to recognize genius is to be dull indeed, is it not? I had this experience reviewing a recent novel by a moderately well-known writer. As a matter of fact I was inclined to favor her book, having read excerpts in a magazine and liked them. But after finishing the whole novel I realized it set enormous goals and failed to achieve them. The book turned out to be the focus of a good advertising campaign; other reviews appeared and were for the most part favorable. I considered retiring and taking up horticulture. First, though, I went back to the book dispassionately, my review already in print. It was still unsuccessful, and I was glad to have said so.

For one learns, after much time and ink and struggle, that there are no absolute standards of literary accomplishment, especially today when traditional and experimental modes rightfully flourish side by side. Reviewers' opinions will vary as much as readers'; the difference is that reviewers are expected to have the skill to articulate clearly what they think and why they think it. That is the most, in all conscience, that one can do, and it is no small task. Once it is done, let the reader be left to his own devices.

GEORGE A. WOODS is the Editor for Children's Books, *The New York Times Book Review*. He is the author of two books, *Vibrations* (1970) and *Catch a Killer* (1972) both published by Harper & Row.

6

Reviewing Books for Children

by GEORGE A. WOODS

THIS YEAR the thought will occur to perhaps a thousand housewives or their husbands, an equal number of frustrated but still aspiring journalism or library school graduates and legions of children (having been encouraged by their teachers) that they all can and should be writing reviews of children's books for *The New York Times Book Review*.

Their confidence grows when they consider the picture book. The text is seemingly simple, often repetitive; words are basic and comprehensible; plots are uncomplicated. The older among these would-be reviewers get further reassurance from the fact that it hasn't been that long since they were sitting on mama's or grandma's lap, being read to, and they have acute, nostalgic recollections of those happy times.

For the recent graduates, journalism in particular, it's a place to start, a marketplace for their talents, but most assuredly only temporary because it's a form of baby talk and one does grow up and out of it.

The youngest among those suddenly inspired by the

thought of becoming critics, the bright junior and senior high school students, are also excited by the prospect of combat against the adult literary establishment that has for years been dictating their scholastic and recreational reading. Here is a chance to strike back, even to wrest control.

And for all of those groups mentioned there is the final, clinching argument: maybe the impressive words or bright phrases to use in evaluating the latest adult best seller are elusive, but nothing in the children's world is beyond their ken. Besides, it's not exactly alien territory; they were children once themselves.

A good many of those adults and young people will send a letter to *The Times* offering their services as reviewers. The students will demand it as their inalienable right. A majority of the adults will begin with "Dear Madam" or "To Whom It May Concern," not taking the trouble to learn the name of the editor. Some will wonder if *The Times* does "cover" children's books, and, if such is indeed the case, "Please send a book as a trial run." Most of their letters will be politely answered with "Your interest in *The Times* and in children's books is sincerely appreciated, but I regret that at the moment I have no openings on my reviewing staff. Your letter, however, will be kept on file and if an opening occurs I will contact you."

A few, perhaps two dozen a year, are answered more encouragingly because the editor, reading on or between the lines, detects a sincerity, a kind of informality, an innocence or professionalism, but most important, an ability to communicate. The letter to them requests additional information such as: Previous writing experience? What age groups would you like to contend with? Picture books? Have you had any experience with art appreciation? Teen-age novels? What have you read lately that appeals to you? Biographies, perhaps? History? Poetry? Are you willing to rewrite? What is your familiarity with the entire field?

The subsequent answers, if any, are not often encouraging. It is a revelation to the letter writers that children's books come in so many varieties. Life never used to be so complicated.

What has been mentioned thus far is not an exaggerated description designed to amuse. Surely no one reading this chapter would be so callow or insensitive as to repeat those mistakes. Nor is it an exaggeration to say that the world of children's books is complicated and complex. It is, moreover, a multimillion-dollar a year business. Fortunes, as well as reputations, are at stake every semi-annual publishing season. A publishing house's juvenile book editor's continued employment with that firm, as well as that of the children's book staff, can very well hinge upon the reviews accorded his or her books in any one season. Too many bad reviews and consequently too much red ink in the year-end ledger bespeaks a cutting off of heads. In short it is not play school but the world of big business. It follows then that first and foremost a reviewer must have integrity and a conscience and a deep sense of responsibility.

It must be clearly understood here that what we are talking about is the approach of one newspaper, *The New York Times*, and one editor's very personal attitude and approach to the reviewing of children's books. Without writing an autobiography, suffice to say it represents twenty years of direct contact with children's books and reviewing. Other review media may on occasion run a more literate or entertaining review, perhaps cover more books, but for consistency and accuracy, for finding a short-cut to the best children's books currently available, *The New York Times* cannot be beaten. An editor's arrogance? No. It is simply belief in the integrity of one's reviewers and oneself, belief in judgments and decisions freely arrived at using a calm, rational approach.

And now to explain that approach. The vast majority of children's books published are sold to schools and libraries. More than 80 percent is the generally accepted figure. The busy season for bookstore sales of children's books is at Christmas. Despite this imbalance, the orientation of *The Times'* children's book columns is not toward schools and libraries, obviously where the market is. We leave that to other review media—*School Library Journal, The Horn Book, Booklist* and others. Librarians, of course, do use *The Times'* recommendations as a supplementary opinion in their purchases, but we do not consciously attempt to influence their buying habits.

Nor does *The Times* operate in a rarefied literary atmosphere. We are a newspaper reaching some two million people every Sunday. The audience for children's book reviews is, then, the same that the rest of *The Times* reaches—a diverse cross-section of Americans here and abroad, in New York City and across the continent, people in all occupations, in all walks of life.

To narrow it down still further, let us consider the particular section, the *Book Review*. It is read by people curious about books, who care about literature, who are concerned with news of the book world and trends, who are inveterate readers of the classics as well as best sellers. Further refined, the audience, then, for the children's columns is the same as the one that reads the rest of the *Book Review*.

But here the situation becomes more complicated and troublesome for the editor directly bearing the responsibility for children's reviews. It can be a very humbling experience to take stock and realize that one handles only a few columns in a substantially sized section of a many-sectioned, extremely large Sunday newspaper. No one can possibly read everything in the Sunday *Times*. People are selective. Although as editors we take pride in the total package, the big, bulky Sunday newspaper, as well as the daily paper, we are competitive with one another for people's interest, and yes, affection. Surely, we think, ours is the most important section in the paper. There is even jealousy. I know that I am resentful over the space accorded adult mysteries, science fiction, how-to books, even letters to the editor. But just as not everything that is news can be accommodated within the news sections, not every book can be reviewed. Decisions must be made every week by the *Book Review* editor, who can please no one completely for very long, passed down the line to specific editors for their further painful decisions as to what book or books will have to be passed over.

Which children's books shall be reviewed? There are 2,000 new ones every year. The space afforded permits perhaps 400 to be reviewed. This is where my personal philosophy enters. To begin with, I want something for the child, not a specific child but the universal child without regard to color, condition, religion, or origin. I want the best books for the most children. Consider: their books are written, edited, produced, promoted, reviewed, sold, and purchased by adults. The child is seldom if ever considered directly. Someone has to be his advocate amid all the brassy, shiny gloss published each year. He doesn't have purchasing power. He is helpless, all too often a victim. And so the child is my most important consideration. Will the book be comprehensible to him? Will it bring his emotions into play? Will it show him other places, other ways, worlds he never dreamed existed?

How does one reach the child? The child does not read the reviews; adults do. But do adults care? Their record, on the surface, is not good when you remember that 20 percent or fewer purchase books through bookstores. More plastic toys are purchased. Can one reasonably expect a middle-income family to lay out the price of today's books?

I am aware of all these difficulties. Many of the problems besetting children's books can be attributed to ignorance and economics. But perhaps most important, we haven't tried hard enough. We have let the home purchase of books go by default. Publishers share some of this blame by having concentrated their promotional efforts on schools and libraries and at conventions. And, lacking a body of disciplined criticism, we have been too adulatory in extolling the shoddy and the mediocre.

I believe that every year there are some books, perhaps only a mere handful, that are a child's rightful heritage. These are books that a child can truly call his own, truly love, want to possess, to grow up with as strongly as he does with any stuffed teddy or security blanket. He may not instinctively recognize those books, may push them aside physically, but they are forever part of his mind and eye. They have made an indelible impression.

And so that is the reviewer's task, my task, too, to go through a winnowing process, casting out, holding onto, separating, ever narrowing, trying to bring those precious few books and all of those children together, with the parent as an instrument or intermediary. Therefore, it is the parent who must be seduced, intrigued by the prospect of a child owning a book.

The parent must first be enticed into reading the children's book columns. His is a busy world. He unconsciously proportions his time; there is just so much time to be allotted to the newspaper. After all, there is television with its pernicious hold. As he leafs through the Sunday *Times*, he may be tempted to pass over the children's reviews; after all, he thinks, they are of no concern to him. Perhaps an illustration will arrest his attention. Perhaps if he pauses long enough to read an opening line, the lead sentence, he may be intrigued. That's what we want, a snappy, succinct few words that should reach out, grab him as a lure to a fish. Play upon his weaknesses; let us say, for instance, like most parents, all he knows is Dr. Seuss, the name, the books. Let us postulate as a lead sentence, "I hate Dr. Seuss." The review could very well be in praise of a particular Dr. Seuss book, but the lead will make him stop to consider his own position. A sentence that is fast, hard, terse, direct is what is needed.

But now for something apparently contradictory. The lead sentence can be wordy. This opening line for a review of Bernard Waber's picture book, *Lovable Lyle*, about a crocodile with very human propensities: "Ordinarily I don't like crocodiles; they're reptilian and bumpety and slithery all over." There you have a very personal approach, informal, nothing pretentious, sharing a very human response. The chance reader's curiosity, we hope, was piqued.

A review that begins with "Here is a good book" is going nowhere. It is not going to attract attention in this world of seductive attractions, nor is any opening sentence that attempts to impress the reader with the reviewer's erudition. We are at a late stage in the development of literature; no one is going to say anything that hasn't been said before. One hopes, however, that the reviewer will say it in his own way, differently, with his own wit, in his own words, with wisdom. A satisfactory lead sentence may very well take hours to compound. Very few of us have instant genius.

Ideally, a review should consist of two substantial paragraphs, one of plot condensation or a description of the book's contents. Summarizing or condensing is often a stumbling block. The beginner insists on providing every detail, every nuance. Strive for the essence. Ask yourself what is the kernel, the nut, the very inner core, and put it into a one-sentence description. Too often the beginner describes a picture book in more words than the author himself has used in writing the story. Pages have been written in overanalyses of Ezra Jack Keats' *The Snowy Day*. Essentially, it is a story of a little boy's first experiences with the wonders of snow. He tracks in it, lies in it, slides in it, and, like all little boys, is soaked by it. To overdescribe the simple wondrous account is an invasion of the author's creative province. Stick to the essentials, the bold outline. Do not overelaborate.

The second paragraph should be a critique. This should be devoted to how the reviewer felt about the book, its interest, appeal, the characters, what special virtues the book has or lacks. The temptation is to say, "I liked this book very much"—but much more is required. Exactly as one has reduced the plot construction to its essence, so one has to pare down the verbosity of criticism. There is much to praise, much with which to take issue. You can be a shuttlecock: on the one hand this, on the other hand that, leaving the review reader in a quandary. He will wonder what you really do believe or if you even know your own mind. Score a point, light somewhere, be decisive, no matter how painful. Be a guide, help the prospective purchaser. Do not vacillate. The buck stops with you. You did want to be a reviewer, didn't you? Indeed, "uneasy lies the head that wears a crown."

This second paragraph is more difficult than the first. There is no longer a plot to paraphrase. The writer is on his own, looking into his own heart, his own soul. He has embarked on a search for truth. If he is slick, glib or clever at someone else's expense (the author or the illustrator), rest assured he will be found out and exposed. Remember, someone is weighing those words, being hurt, being pleased. And somewhere an editor is evaluating your worth to the cause of an enduring body of literature and criticism.

The particular format already mentioned is only a suggestion for the beginner. With experience and practice, one learns how to interweave description and critique skillfully. There should be a continual striving for perfection and improved technique. As no two books are completely alike, each one presenting its own separate challenge, the reviewer cannot fall back on the same comfortable formula each time. Reviewing is an art form unto itself and a demanding assignment every time.

It will be asked where do *The Times* reviewers come from? They are as diverse as the authors who write the books. Most often I use authors, authors whom I admire for something special in their work or for a particular book. Barbara Wersba, Natalie Babbitt, Georgess McHargue, Judith Viorst, for instance. I hasten to add that merely because I happen to admire their talent and use their services is not any guarantee that their books will necessarily be reviewed or even reviewed favorably. Quite the reverse; in fact, not reviewing their books on occasion, or reviewing them unfavorably has been embarrassing and has sometimes strained professional relations. Most reviewers, however, are professionally tactful enough not to mention any imagined violence done to their creative efforts.

I always avoid using as a reviewer an author whose previous book or even work-in-progress might be competitive with the book under review. I also try to avoid mixing reviewers and authors from the same publishing house. Sometimes I may err in my selection, but I do have confidence in the integrity of each reviewer I choose.

Authors, I find, are most suitable as reviewers because they are devoted to the field, are part of it, have made contributions, know the problems, the genre, are interested in bringing about improvements in the quality of the reading fare offered young people. They also know the problems of writing and are in the business of communicating. Poets, too, I find, make excellent reviewers. They tend to create, they reach for words, describe with a special richness and beauty. They also write with a certain precision and terseness.

Where nonfiction books are concerned, I tend to seek out experts in the field. If a volume concerns some form of wildlife, I might use a curator from the Bronx Zoo; if on the universe, then perhaps someone from a planetarium; if on history, then some professor from our many universities. On the other hand, if the book is formidable and technical, I might be perverse enough to send it to a layman. After all, if a child is to read and understand the book, what better choice than a mere mortal as a reviewer?

Here it is important that I mention I abhor cruelty in a review. I realize that a book is an extension of its author. It is his good right arm or leg. All authors have heard the applause of the crowd in their minds while writing their books, have dreamed of medals and acclaim. They have done their best. I will not permit their work to be made sport of, to be kicked and gouged, trampled upon. A simple, graceful bit of negative criticism will do. So don't belabor a putdown; don't rip and slash and snort and tear.

I do have a tendency to favor illustrious names among the authors of adult books, those very often without any familiarity of the children's book world. Irresponsible? Two goals are sought. First, the name of the reviewer attracts attention and readership. People are curious to know what a John Hersey, John Updike, Eudora Welty or a Reynolds Price thinks about a particular book or group of books. Readers are likely to be impressed that a famous name in the world of literature would deign to be concerned with books for children.

There are contemptuous attitudes toward children's books. I have always found this curious, but it is a sad fact that there are adults, all too many, who feel that children's books are, if not quite illegitimate, then at best, poor, remote, ugly stepchildren. This attitude is quite prevalent among authors of adult literature. When approached to write a children's book review (even though the payment is commensurate with that for adult books), they refuse with a disdainful snicker, an I'm-awfully-busy-right-now, or I-don't-know-anything-about-children's-books.

The latter response is the easiest to deal with. The reply is: you were a child once; perhaps you have children of your own, at least a niece or nephew; know a neighbor's child. You don't have to condescend; just ask yourself if you'd like them to read and have this book. We have the same high standards as for reviewing adult books and use no baby talk. Once they are reassured, they find the task most always a pleasurable assignment that broadens their knowledge and the base of appeal for children's books.

The snicker is harder to handle, difficult to combat but not impossible. But why this attitude? It may be historical. If you go back far enough into the newspaper files and read what passed for criticism, you'll see why. There was little harshness, no outright condemnation of a book's inadequacy. The meanest statement made about a children's book was that it was just short of terrific. There was a reason for all this. With so little space afforded books for young readers, the editors at the time felt it did not warrant utilizing precious space to be negative. Sour, dour, and doubtful reviews languished on the editor's desk and died of old age without ever seeing the light of print. Consequently, an imbalance was created in the prospective book purchaser's mind. Everything seemed perfect in the children's world. And if they bought any of those innocent, colorfully appealing books, then as now, they could have been subject to if not bafflement then a major disappointment. Burned too many times, they stayed clear of any further involvement with those products. Best to leave it to the librarians, they may have felt.

Today it is important that success and failure in literature be registered in print. Children's books are no less immune to scrutiny and appraisal than adult books. And it should be pointed out that the proportion of the good to the bad is the same in children's books as in adult books.

There should be no thought of journalistic censorship except for extreme cases where a reviewer has failed hopelessly to express himself with clarity. If a reviewer knows that an editor publishes reviews of only positive and praiseworthy books, he may seek to exercise his vanity out of a desire to see his name in print and promptly. In short, he will think and praise in more positive terms than a book warrants. Therefore, it is incumbent upon an editor to print what he gets. I often print reviews of books with which I do not agree, but I have asked for a written opinion and feel compelled to publish it. Not thy will but the reviewer's be done.

It is not a pleasing prospect to be churlish, difficult to please, irascible, in print. It is always more difficult to damn than to praise. If a reviewer takes issue with a book, he has to be precise, to prove his case, and to point, document, get down and root around in his mind for precisely what is out of whack, lacking or wrong in the book. Rest assured, he will hear from the author or the publishing house editor. They do not take responsible criticism, let alone irresponsible criticism, lightly. On the other hand, if a reviewer writes reams of praise, touts the wonders and marvels of a particular book, he or she will join the ranks of the much beloved. Of course he may not be too happy with himself if he has praised only to avoid angry retorts.

But let us return to the choice of reviewers. I have mentioned authors of juvenile and adult books, poets, experts in their fields. There are others. Teachers, librarians, parents, artists, former publishing house editors, the proverbial butchers, bakers, and candlestick makers, anyone who I think can do the job of appraising and communicating. But make no mistake: Again, I repeat that those are hard, demanding, exacting words. If I ask for 200 words, I guarantee that these will be some of the hardest 200 words that person has ever produced. You may be asked to rewrite, to clarify, to point up; you may be asked "what do you mean by this phrase or that line," either on the telephone or in a letter. Or you may not hear from me for several months and, being too terrified to contact me because I am awesome and formidable, imagine that you have failed dismally. And then one day, lo and behold, there is your work in print. O frabjous day. But just because you have been printed once does not make it certain that you will be printed again. Attribute it to my whimsicality, business, forgetfulness or that you caused me too much trouble in the editing. On the other hand, you may receive another book to review in a few months. Nothing is certain, and I am under no obligation to anyone —editor, author, artist, review writer—only to the child.

Now my own part as a reviewer. One of the benefits of being the editor is having first choice, selecting the books I review myself. Are you envious? Don't be. Like anyone else, I have a lazy streak. I try to avoid unnecessary expenditure of energy. Writing can be rewarding, but it can also be a prison, a term of confinement to be served at the typewriter. And, contrary to what many people believe, writers do not think in complete sentences, let alone complete paragraphs. It is the laborious task of compounding one word upon another, striking out, beginning again, changing, giving up in disgust, of discouragement with oneself. It can be an exquisite torture, a form of professional analysis, the rack, the stocks, bondage. You work and hear the sound of laughter, of glasses clinking, of music, gunshots on TV, dream of a tropical island where there is nothing to do but loll in the sun, pick the accumulated gunk out of the letter "e" on your typewriter (the letters "a," "b," "p," "d" seem to be quite prone to dirt, and don't forget the capitals and the numerals), dust underneath the typewriter, think of a hundred minor household projects that require immediate attention. But then there are deadlines and the self-accusation of cowardice.

Other than the outright desire of avoidance, I do have a nine-to-five job requiring attention to editing, letter writing, proofreading and self-indulgence. I also have to spend a large portion of my day in previewing, looking at every book that comes into the office. Some days I may read fifteen or twenty books, other days none. Not all of them are an unmitigated pleasure to read; some are worse than others. Prolonged exposure to them produces despondency. But still I read and weed, discard what I think is of less merit, save some that I hope might be coupled with another book on the same subject that I know will be forthcoming. Some I know I will have to send out for review, even though I am not satisfied with the content, because the book is by someone famous, perhaps a former Newbery, Caldecott, National Book Award winner, a prominent adult writer. In short, they have news value, even if not child satisfaction.

There are some books I have to read very little in. I have been on the scene for quite awhile, know almost instinctively various authors' capabilities, judging by their past performances. I read just enough of a book to reassure myself that I am not being prejudiced against them. But then, perhaps on the next book I pick up and begin reading, something happens . . . time stops, I am there, in that book, in that exact place as the author has described it. I am afraid or elated, laughing or crying. I am responding. I resent intrusions from those around me, find that I cannot afford the luxury of office time for indulging myself in pure pleasure or excitement. I take the book home with me, finish it. I have become part of that book, and it has become part of me, forever inseparable. It is a kind of love affair.

And like all love affairs, there has to be a confiding, a telling, yes, a shouting from the rooftops. And who will do that? But wait—suppose the one who does the shouting doesn't understand my new-found affection; doesn't believe it, mocks my find? Then I must do it myself, because I dare not run the risk of having anyone else break the news, consider it unimportant, not stress certain facts. Yes, I will have to do it.

That is much the way it works. I do what moves me, what makes me laugh or cry, what excites me, impresses me with its power and imagery, what is literate, new, beautiful, meritorious, provocative, profound; what is majestic, is not vile or vulgar. All of those things, but perhaps best summed up by something less romantic and impressive. In short, what boils down to the moment when my head and heart and stomach, too, all cooperate with the print before my eyes.

The task now is to capture those feelings in words, put them down on paper logically, coherently, appealingly, not to go overboard as on some first love affair. There must be a sense of proportion, a checking and rechecking of one's emotions and intelligence. It is not *War and Peace*, not *Charlotte's Web*, or *Sylvester and the Magic Pebble*, but what is it?

The plot must be distilled, condensed; it must be succinct, intelligible; the review must read swiftly, brightly, eruditely. Make no mistake. I need a first sentence. Where are you, muse? Nothing will come. I may spend days going to and from work driving the car and thinking of a lead sentence, the right sentence; go to bed thinking of a concluding or wrap-up sentence, something the reader will take away with him if nothing else. It may mean days of intermittent thinking about a character or a situation. How do I express it as best I possibly can?

And then it's done. The parts are joined. Finished? No, not really; nothing is ever really finished. One always worries over the review as over a new baby, wondering if it really is the best, the prettiest baby ever born, wondering if I am too enthusiastic, a bore, right or wrong. Have I done my job? One seeks after absolute justice in this world for oneself. So why not for others?

And yet, and yet, there is a strong subjective element in any review. There is no objective yardstick that one can place against a book and say, "The good stick says this does not measure up." Good or bad, success or failure is measured largely in the reviewer's responses and mind. I think of John Donovan's *Wild in the World*, which was reviewed intentionally in *The Times* by two eminent critics in two separate reviews running on the same page on the same Sunday. One said it was the worst book ever written for young people; the other said it was the finest book ever written for young people. Who was right? Who was wrong?

There is that one final reward to reviewing, at least for me, and I would imagine for anyone. After more than twenty years and thousands of books reviewed, the thrill is still there. I still get a kick out of seeing my name in print.

WILLIAM MCPHERSON received the Pulitzer Prize
for Distinguished Criticism in 1977. He is editor
of *The Washington Post* "Book World," where
parts of this chapter first appeared.

7

The Book Reviewer's Craft

by WILLIAM MCPHERSON

IT CAME to my attention the other day that a much respected
academic critic recently said, about a genuinely illuminating
article on one of the important novels of our time, that no
serious journal would publish it: "it's merely appreciation"—
in the academy a dread, dismissive word. But book reviewing
at its best is just that—"merely appreciation."

A lot of writers would settle for—and some of the worst
demand—appreciation, by which they mean love and praise.
(They forget that it is possible to love the culprit while de-
ploring the crime, and our best advice to them is to take their
money and run, laughing, as they say, to the bank or the
psychiatrist.) But appreciation as defined in *Webster's Third*
is another category of recognition. To appreciate is "to judge
or evaluate the worth, merit, quality, or significance of; to
comprehend with knowledge, judgment, and discrimination. . . . *Appreciate* connotes recognition of worth or merit
through wise judgment, analytical perception, and keen
insight." This being the real world, we could argue endlessly

68

and ultimately pointlessly as to whose judgments are wise, whose analyses perceptive, whose insights keen. Time (with luck) will tell.

Appreciation, of course, is not affirmation; meretricious junk remains meretricious junk, no matter how cleverly disguised or on what level. It is important to recognize it, to appreciate it, but *not* to affirm it. An acquaintance suggested recently that "affirming" books are denied good notices because of some defect of vision in reviewers, rather than any defect in the book itself. (He had just published what I believe he considered such a book. It was not praised. Therefore, reviewers are blind.) Although I have only a vague idea of what an "affirming" book might be (presumably one that makes us feel good, is sanguine and optimistic), I have a dark suspicion that I wouldn't like it, thus confirming my friend's conviction that reviewers come out of the factory with a defective part, perhaps a harpoon where the heart ought to be, or several shriveled cells in the head.

Making us feel comfortable is not a primary function of literature; sand in an oyster may produce a pearl but it irritates the oyster. So it is with books, which give us pleasure not because they make us comfortable, though some good ones may, but because they entertain us, they make us laugh, they make us cry; they inform, persuade, disturb, convince, seduce us; they make us think, speculate, see— and we recognize what we see as true, not as *the* truth but as a truth in the writer's fabulous construction that corresponds to what we have observed in ourselves, or others, or in the world at large, or can conceive of observing. The writer's Sisyphean task—the task of every human being, in fact—is to take the discrete sensations the world provides in bewildering number and complexity and forge them, within the limits of his time and space, into a coherent reality that can be dealt with. Art is indeed metamorphosis.

Reviewers—or at least this reviewer—are only too happy to affirm the above, although affirmation by itself is no positive good. *Jonathan Livingston Seagull* might be considered a very "affirming" book, but it's not the reviewer's duty to praise it. More important to consider what is being affirmed, whether the ideas, the words, the vision are trite, stupid, self-serving, banal, or brilliant. The artist may celebrate; the reviewer must cogitate, scrutinize, analyze, tell us what the book is trying to do, how it's doing it, if it succeeds. If a book is meant only to entertain, then the review should answer the question, is it entertaining? It is not fair to ask a reviewer to "affirm" a book simply because the book seems positive. We do ask that he affirm the value of reading in a society where reading matters less and less.

John Updike, in his foreword to *Picked-Up Pieces* (Knopf, 1975), lists five rules for writing a book review. They are simple, practical and good, and eminently worth not only repeating but inscribing on a reviewer's stony heart. Mr. Updike's first rule is, "Try to understand what the author wished to do, and do not blame him for not achieving what he did not attempt." (Peter Benchley, when he wrote *Jaws*, wasn't trying for *Moby Dick*.) Updike's second rule is to give enough direct quotation from the book so that the reader can form his own impression of the author's style and sensibility. Third and fourth, avoid extended plot summaries; don't attempt a précis but describe the book with the help of selective short quotations from it. Fifth, if the book fails, cite a successful example of its kind. "Try to understand the failure," Updike writes. "Sure it's his and not yours?" Then, of course, there is the matter of integrity: don't accept a book for review that you are already committed to like (because the author is your best friend) or to despise (because he was your best friend until he seduced your wife). "Do not imagine yourself a caretaker of any tradition, an enforcer of any party standards, a warrior in any ideological battle, a corrections officer of any kind," Updike writes. "Review the book, not the reputation. Submit to whatever spell, weak or strong, is being cast. Better to praise and share than blame and ban." Then, I would add, have the strength of your convictions: pull no punches but be prepared for a pummeling; authors are notoriously, justifiably sensitive, and opinions dismayingly subjective.

Rules, of course, are easier to make than to follow. Lofty abstractions possess a kind of Platonic purity that isn't found in the imperfect world in which we live and work and write—all against time, as it were. In this world, our readers are asking a simple but legitimate question, the question any reader asks first: "Should I read this book, spend my time on it, my money for it?" To answer it, a simple yes or no is not enough. A book review section is more than a shopper's guide; a good one is also a news medium, a reference source, a place where ideas are disseminated, and a journal with some pretentions to literacy, wit and seriousness. It assumes a reader with at least as much intelligence as the reviewer and the editor, and that the reader wants to be shown *how* the reviewer thinks about the book, not told *what he* should think about it. So a better question for the reader to ask is, "Should I pay any attention to this review?" Based on his own interests, intelligence and time, but based most of all on his evaluation of the review, the reader thus makes up his own mind, becoming, in effect, the reviewer's reviewer, evaluating the pleasure (or pain) of the text he is reading and, by extension, the potential pleasures of the text he is reading about. If the reviewer is any good, he will provide the context for the reader's decision about the book; if he's not, he'll provide, however unwittingly, the basis for a decision on the review.

Most reviewers in journalism—which is most of us, writing the kind of reviews most of us read—are more inclined to praise too lavishly than to criticize too stringently. A reader of so many books, so many of them less than interesting, seizes on what crumbs he can, and sometimes mistakes a cream puff for more solid fare. That is why it is necessary, every now and then, for a reviewer to put aside next week's book and look at one that has stood up over time. Judgments without standards are empty indeed. And judgments themselves are less interesting—and more dubious—than the process by which they are arrived at; just as in reading it is the process that pleasures us, or fails to, and later the memory of it. To say a book is "unforgettable" or "a masterpiece"—both of which, I regret to confess, I have in greener days said and may in a future indiscretion repeat—is to say very little. But to suggest how a book is put together, why it works or fails to work, to demonstrate its accuracy or reveal its errors, to bring some illuminating insight to the whole, is to say a great deal—especially in a thousand words. If, in addition, a reviewer tells us with seeming careless ease something about how the language works, how our minds work, and how society works while keeping his focus on the book in question, you have the best in book reviewing. Call it "merely appreciation"—but with discernment, discrimination, illumination.

LARRY SWINDELL has been book editor of *The Philadelphia Inquirer* since 1972. He is also the author of three motion picture biographies, the most recent of which is *Screwball: The Life of Carole Lombard* (Morrow).

8

The Function of a Book Editor

by LARRY SWINDELL

THE BOOK review section of any newspaper or magazine inevitably reflects a book editor's taste, his perspective on books—as commerce or literature or both—and something of his reviewing philosophy.

I review a new book almost every Sunday in *The Philadelphia Inquirer*, but other book editors review irregularly, and some choose not to review at all. Many book editors confine their own writing to chatty columns about the book scene, gleaned from author interviews and meetings with book people. Yet all of us are catalysts for the book reviews that inhabit the pages for which we're responsible.

When I became book editor of *The Inquirer* several years ago, I accepted as gospel what I had heard: that a book editor's most important responsibility is to determine which books will be reviewed. That is an important judgment, but it no longer has the highest priority in my own management of book reviews. It is more important that the book be given to the *right* reviewer. There is no particular honor in having a review of a high-profile book just for the record, if the review is misguided and misguiding for having been mis-assigned. When a book is reviewed by someone unqualified to judge it, or otherwise an injudicious choice for doing so, there is all-around disservice—to the author, to the publishers, to the readers of the review, and also to the reviewer himself.

A book editor must experiment with reviewers to de-termine their individual strengths and weaknesses, their range and limitations, and (often) their unconscious prej-udices. Good judgment does not make a good book reviewer, but the ability to articulate good judgment does. However, some gloriously endowed writers have difficulty making a book review coherent and informative. Others, perhaps more modestly talented, in the course of becoming good book re-viewers, also become accomplished in a specific type of writing. Every kind of writer interested in reviewing should be given a chance by the book editor. Of necessity, there is some trial and error involved, but if the editor's instincts are sound, the mistakes from trying reviewers on speculation will be few and minimal.

We do not—we *should* not—impose our own judgments upon our reviewers, or imply, overtly or even subtly, that we hope to receive a favorable or an unfavorable review of a certain book. Nor should a book editor second-guess a reviewer's assessment to the point of altering it. The book editor should not "control" the reviews; yet ultimately he does that, simply because he controls the assignments.

A book should be reviewed only by someone with honest interest in—preferably, a passion for—reading that specific book. Only in that case, if the reviewer's judgment is nega-tive, can his disappointment in the book be genuine: he en-tertained high expectations that the reading of the book did not fulfill. That is very different from having a reviewer write a thumbs-down review and say, "This just wasn't my cup of tea." The book should have been reviewed by a connoisseur of that blend of tea.

All book editors must contend with the thorny problem of zealous would-be reviewers. For its invitation to personal expression, the book review is an appealing form for just about every denomination of writer. Unfortunately, many free-lance writers seem more eager to review a book than to read one. It is a grave mistake (and I've made it often enough) to assign a book for review to someone who otherwise would have no inclination to read it, but book editors make this error because so many writers respond affirmatively to the most tentative suggestion of a book they might review. However, only by giving would-be reviewers an opportunity to try reviews can the editor assemble a team of review specialists. As editor and reviewer work together in a continuing relationship, each begins to know what the other wants.

Selection

In an ordinary week, I receive about 150 books from publishers interested in having them reviewed in *The Inquirer*. (At a seasonal peak—in September, say—there will be 200 or more a week.) The Sunday book pages of *The Inquirer* are budgeted for no more than eight reviews of varying assigned lengths averaging only 500 words. Therefore, about one in every twenty incoming books is destined for review in the book section. Short of reading all the books, how do I determine which will be reviewed there?

As with a good many other book editors, I have in many cases made the determination long before the book has been received. The trade publishers distribute their catalogues well in advance of their season, and this gives the book editor early opportunity to get a track on some of the more obvious big guns that will be coming. Then, most editors receive *Publishers Weekly* (the trade journal of the book industry), and I also receive the biweekly *Kirkus Reviews*; both of these publications review the major publishers' wares about two months prior to publication date. If a book receives uncommonly enthusiastic endorsement from both sources, I will probably then decide to have the book reviewed. *PW* and *Kirkus* read bound galleys of uncorrected proofs, and enterprising publishers also get early galleys out to the more important book editors. This is a vital accommodation to magazines requiring longer lead time for planning and production. But bound galleys are also useful to newspaper book editors, who can then have time to get an advance "reader report" on a book that may be a borderline case for reviewing.

When those 150 books arrive in a typical week, perhaps half a dozen are already scheduled for review, and the reviews may already have been assigned. Although it seems from this that only two are to be selected for review from the remaining 144 books, this figure is deceptive. When we make an early decision to review certain books, we at the same time decide in advance against reviewing many others of those received. Also, plans may already have been made for handling certain of these books elsewhere in the newspaper. For example, some sports books will go to the sports department, business books to the business editor, cookbooks to the food writers, and so on. In their own columns, they'll feature books in articles that will contain review elements and have the *effect* of a review. As many as two dozen books may be distributed on this basis in any given week.

The main attention of the book section is devoted to

fiction and nonfiction of general interest and wide appeal. The Sunday circulation of 900,000 presumes perhaps 2,000,000 readers, and while the book section captures only a small percentage of the paper's readership, an estimated 250,000 persons do read it every week. For the most part, those readers are a specialized group with definite literary interests, so the section cannot cover only the commercial bread-and-butter of the book industry. That "commercial" extreme on the one hand and the "ivory tower" on the other must both be accommodated, but the primary emphasis must be on new books somewhere between the two extremes. The scope of a newspaper book section is rather different from the concerns of a literary quarterly.

Hence, I may be screening no more than two dozen books to decide on two for possible review. That is not a difficult or time-consuming chore. In only a few minutes, a book editor can learn a lot about any book. If it is a work of non-fiction, he can scan the preface and learn about the author's objectives and the book's scope. A book editor also learns to read between the lines of jacket-copy puffery. In fiction particularly, a few paragraphs of a novel can convey a sense of the author's style and perhaps his point of view.

When I actually get to examine a book that tentatively has made the review schedule, I may change my mind and remove it, or add one not originally selected for review. Instead of the budgeted eight, I may have ten or twelve books eligible for review, and decide to assign "conditional" reviews in the marginal cases. More likely, however, the eight books will be selected on the basis of my ability to match the book with a qualified and enthusiastic reviewer. Sometimes I am unable to do this, but that does not mean the book can't be reviewed in *The Inquirer*. I have a purchase option on any of John

Markham's reviews (a syndicated reviewing service), and his service becomes a valuable backup for books for which suitable reviewers eluded me, and in those occasional cases in which I underestimated the book when I screened it. Just as my own reviews are circulated by the Knight Newspaper wire services, so am I in a position to use reviews filed through wire services my paper subscribes to. Still, more than ninety percent of the reviews appearing in *The Inquirer* are assigned by me.

In half a dozen years, I have collected an ever-growing stable of reviewers, some of whom are in extremely specialized fields and contribute rarely, while others cannot be given as many assignments as they would like. The current roster includes 200 free-lance reviewers, exclusive of *Inquirer* staff members, who supply about 40 percent of the reviews, on a free-lance basis. This is not a rigid formula, it is just the way it works out; the staff is a valuable resource, especially for their expertise in many areas of nonfiction. The "outside" reviewers may be other professional journalists, editors, and authors; they may be educators—usually university professors with scholarly credentials, for books of literary interest; or they may represent unrelated fields. Some of my reviewers are housewives, who are superbly educated and trained, and have kept up with new books. All of them must meet a reviewing standard that is meant to be always rising; when they can't, benign neglect is the primary technique for cutting them adrift.

Some reviewers cut themselves adrift, for their unreliability with deadlines, or for their tendency to turn in a 2,000-word critical essay as opposed to a 500-word review. Walter Kerr once defined the difference between a review and a piece of criticism as the difference between a work that is being introduced to the reader and a work with which the reader's familiarity is assumed. Many reviewers seem unable to grasp this difference, but they must.

I know very few writers who can take on any kind of book and review it professionally, fairly, and well. Every one of my reviewers becomes some kind of specialist in my own scheme of things, even though some have occasion to exhibit considerable range within their specialized areas. Some of them review only nonfiction, others only fiction, and a few do both, but almost always with a pronounced leaning toward one or the other. My own inclination is toward fiction, yet I review nonfiction about as often, but in a limited sphere: popular history, literary biography, and such subjects as movies and even baseball. I'm envied for having first choice of all the forthcoming books, and I do consciously select a good many books that are assured of becoming household-word titles. The newspaper expects me to give personal attention to the "important" books; consequently, my own reviews often take the "lead" position—headlined and illustrated—but not always.

For all the advance planning that goes into a book review section, the decision on what book will have the lead position, which ones will get a moderately good play, and which will be relatively "buried" must depend on these final considerations: the stature of the book as established by the review; the prominence of the author or the subject; and the readability of the review as original commentary and original writing. Again, the composition of the book pages, the types of books reviewed, and even the tone and style of the reviews reflect the book editor's views of life and literature.

In my role as catalyst, I try to display some logic and even some idealism to transcend any personal idiosyncrasies. *The Inquirer* is one of the very few newspapers presently committed to the encouragement of fiction, particularly new fiction. By that I do not mean "new writing" with the *avant-garde* spirit that those words imply, but fiction by authors either completely unknown or as yet unestablished.

Contrary to many watchers of the book scene, I believe we are in an age of abundant good fiction, but that a large segment of its potential readership is denied the knowledge of its existence by some critics, who have created a barrier between their own interests and the public's. Critics almost always have been in the literary mainstream and have a kinship with enlightened readers of fiction. There was always an *avant-garde,* and customarily it served a valuable function in keeping the literary establishment off balance, or at least on its toes. But now the *avant-garde* has become the literary/critical establishment, its attention to "new writing" having produced an inbred community. Writers are now producing fiction not for readers who enjoy novels, but for other writers and certain critics, or perhaps only for themselves. Many intelligent readers of fiction feel alienated by the critics, who try to force them away from their natural responses. Good writing is one thing, but good reading may be something else; confusing the two has created obstacles to the emergence of the traditional novel that most mature readers would prefer.

I do not mean the genre novels. Good or bad, the Gothics, the murder mysteries, the science fiction speculations, and the raunchy stories about oversexed Beautiful People will always find an audience. But there is a quorum of admirable writers engaged in serious fiction, who do not get the recognition they deserve, and *The Inquirer* does what it can to help bring them to the surface.

Everyone wants to review Bellow and Cheever, Barth and Vonnegut, Roth and Didion and Heller, but finding someone to review, say, some stories by Ann Beattie or even a novel by such a veteran writer as Frederick Buechner, is a challenge. The reviewer should be acquainted with Buechner's or Beattie's past accomplishments. On the other hand, anyone who reads fiction regularly and with discrimination should, it would seem, be equipped to review a first novel, yet it is often as difficult to excite a prospective reviewer's enthusiasm for a first novel as it is to persuade a bookseller to stock one. And not everyone wants to do a preliminary report for us on a first novel that may not be reviewed, even if he is paid for having read the book. Most review fees amount to a modest honorarium anyway, and the reviewer is usually less interested in money than in a by-lined, published review that will enhance his credits. But we usually require a reading of a first novel before a decision on whether or not to review it is made. If the book shows modest achievement or exceptional promise, it deserves to be reviewed, but if it reveals none of these qualities, it should be ignored, because too many worthwhile books compete for recognition within the limited space allotted to book reviews.

Encouragement should be the predominant consideration in reviewing fiction by an unknown or new writer, and I also believe encouragement should be a book review department's primary objective. Of course, a book reviewer is also a kind of readers' consultant, and one must be wary of any reviewer who praises everything. Reviewers should be judicious, they should demand excellence, but above all, they should be fair. Fairness is part of the reviewer's obligation and commitment to search for merit and to celebrate achievement. A negative reading experience should result in a negative review; but the reviewer should take up the book positively, wanting it to succeed—and this is not always the case.

Many of the sample reviews sent to me by hopeful reviewers reveal considerable writing ability, but often their writing talent is revealed only in clever, iconoclastic put-downs of books and authors. In such cases, I cannot take them on; there is a time to damn with faint praise, and there is a time merely to damn, but all damning must be justified. A common weakness of many negative reviews—usually unconscious on the reviewer's part—is an unjustified attack on the author. This is something that must always be deleted from a review. The book editor, functioning as an editor, does not rewrite or distort what the reviewer has presented, but he most certainly can cut. The most fortunate book editors are those whose reviewers' work requires the least amount of editorial attention.

Criteria

So what does a book editor want in a review? I only know what I want, and it may or may not conform to other book editors' criteria. A review must clearly establish itself as personal opinion and must not lose that shading. The writing of the review should be nimble, imaginative, clever; but its primary function is not to call attention to the reviewer or to the writing itself to the point of upstaging the book being reviewed.

Beyond that, no system of rules should dictate "How to Write a Book Review." The book review may well be journalism's last pure and free form of personal expression; certainly it is less monolithic in its format than a film, theatre, or music review. Yet many persons adept at writing in various modes feel confounded by the book review. I have sought out noted educators and respected journalists about reviewing books in their specialized areas, only to have them say that they don't know how to write a book review, having never done it. My response is that if they read books intelligently and can convey their thoughts in the English language, they can review books. Fiction or nonfiction, every book can suggest—and also inspire—the approach, method, and technique of the review.

I have been flattered at times by having persons of prominence within the book publishing or journalistic worlds say that *The Inquirer*'s book section is as good as or even better than any comparable Sunday section. Anyone could have accomplished the same thing, anywhere, merely by giving aspiring reviewers a reasonable chance to show what they can do, and never declaring that there is no more room in the reviewing stable. The greater and more versatile the talent in the stable, the higher the standard may rise. And that can only do good for the world of books.

HERBERT A. KENNY is former book editor of *The Boston Globe* and now runs a literary agency outside of Boston. He continues to do free-lance book reviewing and is the author of several books of poetry. One of the founders of the National Book Critics Circle, he also serves as editor of its *Journal*.

9

The Basics of Book Reviewing

by HERBERT A. KENNY

THERE ARE many generalities that can be stated about book reviewing, and here are a few to begin with. If you are about to write a review, consider whom you are writing it for. The general reader? A college alumnus? This in turn will depend on what audience the author had in mind when he wrote the book you are about to review. Not all books are written for a general audience. Textbooks are designed for students, law books for lawyers, medical books for doctors and science books for the initiated. Indeed, the majority of books are not intended for the majority of readers. For whom is the author writing, and for whom are you writing your review?

The reviewer's job is to tell the reader what the book is about, what the author intends, and how well he achieves his aim. The reviewer reports whether the author writes lucidly and entertainingly. He must also opine whether the average reader (if such a specimen exists) will enjoy the book or whether it is, in effect, worthwhile only for those with a special interest in the subject. Not everyone wants to read about penguins or for that matter DNA unless the material is lucidly presented.

While acknowledging his or her own lack of expertise in a given subject, the reviewer must, nevertheless, be able to tell readers if the author is an authority in the field under discussion and if he represents the majority view, a minority view, or some personal radical view. If the author/authority offers opinions on the applications of his theories, discoveries, or facts to a given social or political situation, the professional reviewer is then permitted to express his dissent or doubts, if dissent or doubts he has. One may defer to a physician on the best way to perform an operation without accepting his opinion on how such surgery should be financed.

In order to do this fairly, the reviewer should take time to familiarize himself with other works by the author and other critical opinions about him. He should also glance at the work of others in the same field. This is true when one is reviewing not only a book in a highly specialized field—say Celtic art—but also a book in other areas, including fiction, even if the reviewer brings solid knowledge to the field. A little humility in the face of the author's accomplishment never hurts. Such preparation also allows the reviewer to strike hard when he determines that a book should be walloped.

A reviewer should try to sympathize with what the author is attempting and give an honest report on what the author is up to before characterizing the work as puerile or perfect, pathetic or powerful, dull or dandy. Too many reviewers approach a review with the intention of making themselves appear bright and sparkling, often at the expense of truth. Equally unacceptable, and at times appalling, is the blunder of attacking the work of a writer because one disagrees with his politics, even though his politics have nothing to do with the work at hand. The reviewer is reviewing the book and not the author, the novel and not the author's life style. As Oscar Wilde pointed out, the fact that a man is a poisoner is nothing against his prose.

The review, in brief, should be addressed to the work at hand. A frequent fault with some reviewers is to chide the author for not having written a different book from the one he has written. The reviewer should review the book for what it purports to be and not denounce the author for having written a book on wit instead of on humor, or the life of Mrs. U. S. Grant instead of Grant himself. The line here is sometimes difficult to draw, for an author can be rightly called to task for canting the book in a direction quite different from what the title and the introduction might lead a reader to believe. The reviewer must always be careful not to slip from criticism (the Greek word meant "to judge") into carping.

These generalities having been stated, how should a book review begin? Like any other popular writing it should begin with phrasing calculated to elicit attention, to catch the eye. Then follow this with examination, explanation, evaluation, and, finally, admiration or condemnation. Interpretation may sometimes be necessary to help the reader understand or appreciate the book.

All this is subject to a Procrustean bed. The reviewer customarily is assigned a definite number of words and must operate in a limited space. To win any editor's heart, trim the review to the precise wordage allotted. Sometimes an editor will appreciate a telephone call telling him that the book in hand merits more words than he has allowed you, but not often. Be on strong ground when you make such a call, and don't consume too much of his time in making your point. The editor has problems that the reviewer knows not of.

How does an unknown writer, never previously published, except perhaps in a school or college publication, go about getting a review published in a major publication and establish himself as a regular reviewer? The question is more easily asked than answered.

What you must do to start is to get published somewhere—in the local weekly newspaper, the local daily, any small regional publication or journal you have access to. Today, many local radio stations will carry an occasional, and sometimes a daily, book review. The best approach of all for the tyro reviewer is to read his or her reviews at some local club meeting. Women's clubs often welcome such speakers (though often without pay) to discuss some recent best seller.

Once you have a fair collection of clippings of your reviews, you can submit them to a book editor with the request that you be given a chance to try doing a review for that editor's literary pages. It is helpful in preparing such reviews if you have a particular specialty in one field or another and ask to review a book related to it. In any event, do not be disturbed or disheartened by refusals. Just keep at it.

You must constantly be refining your own literary style and analyzing the style of reviews published in periodicals for which you'd like to do reviews.

One word of basic advice: You must love books more than you want to use them to make a reputation for yourself as a reviewer. The watchwords are: affection and persistence.

Sample Review

[Some books, though on highly technical subjects, are intended for a general reader. The following is a review I wrote of a science book that was a Book-of-the-Month Club

*selection. My review, as well as the book itself, was aimed at
a general audience—which, it must be understood, is not the
same thing as the mass market. While only a scientist would
be qualified to review such a book for a scientific journal, a
professional book reviewer is the right person to do it for a
general readership. The review first appeared in* The Boston
Globe *and was reprinted in the* Book-of-the-Month Club
News.*—H. A. K.*]

The Roots of Civilization, by Alexander Marshack
McGraw-Hill   413 pp. $17.50
Reviewed by Herbert A. Kenny

Rarely does a book on archaeology come along which reads
like a detective story. One thinks of the decoding of Minoan
Linear B, a major breakthrough in linguistics, but nothing
else. Nothing, that is, to match *The Roots of Civilization,* by
Alexander Marshack, a fellow of the Peabody Museum at
Harvard University, in which he recounts his monumental
breakthrough in understanding paleolithic man.

What he discovered, in brief, is that scratches on bones and
stones more than 30,000 years old which were thought to be
decorative markings or senseless prehistoric doodling are
numerical, calendric notations. Prehistoric man was a "time-
factoring" man. Thus, if we ask ourselves where lie the roots
of our incredible growth of science, here surely are the most
ancient traces, tiny tendrils sunk far back in the dark soil
of lost eons. . . .

More science writer than scientist, Marshack had written a
book on the International Geophysical Year and was writing
one on lunar exploration when curiosity about the remotest
beginnings of science led him to contemplate the Ishango
bone, a 6500 B.C. artifact from the Congo. He could not accept
the markings on it as random scratches or mere decoration.
Some thought it arithmetical notation linked to a counting

system based on ten. That didn't wash either, nor suggest what was being counted. Marshack began to match the markings with the lunar cycles, no easy task in itself. But it worked. How then to prove it to himself and to other scientists?

He moved back in time by more than 20,000 years from the Ishango man and began a critical examination of the artifacts from the Upper Paleolithic Age in Europe. The more pieces he examined the more corroboration he found for his innovative theory. At length his work (begun in 1962) convinced Professor Hallam L. Movius, Jr., of Harvard University, a preeminent authority on the Paleolithic Age. Movius declares that Marshack has achieved "a major breakthrough in the field of the interpretation and understanding of Upper Paleolithic art. . . . These spectacular studies have contributed startlingly new and fundamentally important evidence on the evolutionary level of early man's cognitive and intellectual capacity and on the level of symbolic development he had attained."

The story that Marshack tells has all the cryptographic charm of Edgar Allan Poe's "The Gold-Bug." I don't mean that it is all easy reading because the man who cannot balance a checkbook is going to have difficulty following the arithmetical argument. The difficulty is minimal. The book is written without jargon, since explication is Marshack's forte, and he brings together in a fascinating fusion the relation of prehistoric man, his art, the so-called fertility statuary, the seasons, the lunar cycle, the rutting seasons of wild beasts, the rise and fall of spring floods, the periodicity of women, mythology, ritual and above all the rudimentary beginnings of man's intellectual struggle to seize the world around him and master the nature that at once binds him and gives him life.

GEORGE WARREN is editor of *BooksWest* and author of 33 books. His reviews appear in many publications, in addition to his own, from *American Record Guide* to *Quest/77*.

10

Reviewing at *BooksWest*

by GEORGE WARREN

RECENTLY A bookseller friend of mine, hearing of some of my own activities in the reviewing line, asked me point-blank: "How does one get to be a book reviewer? What are the qualifications?"

The question caught me off balance. My friend is a lady of outstanding expertise in one field—she knows more about the mystery novel than virtually anybody—and she might well make a fine book reviewer in this area. And then again she might not: there are no guarantees.

All I could say, then, was that the qualifications lay mainly in the ability to get somebody, at some journal somewhere, to let you wear the reviewer's hat—and then to get the readers to let you keep it. The poet Goethe said of fiction that the problem it poses is one of getting your reader to let you develop a point of view. This done, you must of course *have* a point of view.

That last, I believe, is the real problem in all writing: point of view. Another word for this is *voice*. Paul Horgan once said that the teacher of writing can do only two things: teach the pupil to find and recognize his own voice and then get out of his way so he can use it.

This approaches being the best statement I ever heard on the subject. What I, as an editor, will be looking for in your copy is your own personal voice, and I—in common with any other editor in the business—will be disappointed if I don't find it. And what I want is the voice that nature, and practice, have given you, not an imitation, however good, of someone you admire.

Every writer worth a hang, on the way to learning his own mind and finding his own voice, tries his hand at imitating his elders and betters. Try it yourself: you'll learn it doesn't work. Exhibit A: Writing a hard-boiled suspense novel in my early years, I remember trying to appropriate a device from James M. Cain. After hours of figurative snipping and pasting, however, I had to admit that the confounded stuff kept going sour until I had written it *my* way.

What did I get out of this kind of experimentation? Only the slowly dawning knowledge, which grew more secure as I went on, that nobody's voice but my own would do, and that when I found that voice I'd better trust it, because it was all I was ever going to have. The same is true with you: If you're going to win any ball games, it's going to be with your own nickel curve and fork ball, not Tom Seaver's smoke. And that's O.K., really: When you've found your own voice and taken the trouble to train it some, it will miraculously become the Almost Perfect Instrument for saying the only things you're ever going to be any good at saying.

As a critic, you'd better learn to be satisfied with that. No apprenticeship you can put in, no education no matter how expensive, is going to do much more for you as a writer.

The process can't be elided, it can't be replaced. You have to live it through. You have to fail at being all those creative people you admire before you can appreciate the value of being yourself—the only person in the world that it's any good at all for you to be—and nobody can save you from the pain of finding this out firsthand.

Try it. Your mind won't *let* you be Edmund Wilson, or Joyce Carol Oates, or Alfred Kazin. You'd love to have Gore Vidal's ear, but you're stuck with your own tin ear. No matter: Your eye may be much better than Vidal's. His, or anybody else's, individual mixture of strengths and weaknesses differentiates him from you absolutely, and you could no more write down to his weaknesses successfully than you could write up to his strengths. You're not only weak in all the wrong places, you're strong in all the wrong places.

Again, you are stuck with being you. Learn to like it. Finding your own voice, with all its flaws, will be the happiest moment of your life and a source of ceaseless joy to you. There is immense dignity—and immense authority—in knowing exactly who you are and what you think about things, and whether you believe this or not right now, your reader will. A strong personal voice is exactly what A. J. Liebling was talking about when he said that, in the last analysis, "The way to write is well, and how you go about it is your own business."

I go into this in some detail because the commonest problem I run into with new reviewers is not one of ignorance. Nor is it one of perception. There are a lot of smart, well-educated people out there, and if intelligence and education were all it took . . . but of course they aren't. The writer has to *sound* like himself; and if he doesn't yet, it just means he isn't ready to do reviews yet, for me or for anyone else.

Of course if he has the right stuff in him, he will tell me and my rejection slip to go whistle up a tree, and he'll go try somewhere else, and he'll keep trying until he *is* ready, and he'll find his acceptance soon enough. Good for him. The one thing all the successful writers I know have in common is not style or talent or any of the usual things you'd expect. It's stubbornness. The real writer is somebody who won't let the world say no to him. The art of reviewing, like all the other arts, is for tough people who believe in themselves. These are the only people hard-headed enough to do everything it takes to find that voice, and train it, and make it work for them.

Train it? How? Well, one of the best ways is to find some way of making your stuff sound the way you speak. The best English, in my book, is based on the spoken word, even if this notion may not be in vogue right now. The truth is that the "literary" prose tends to date, often in a matter of months or years, while the fashion in speech remains pretty much the same. If you want to last, write for the voice.

The market

Now, what else? The review market—the paying one, anyway—does not favor the long-winded writer. It's axiomatic that the only magazines that will, generally, let you waffle along, feeling your way to your point in bumbling first-draft prose, are the ones that pay in copies. The review markets that send checks virtually all require pretty tight writing. This means you're going to have to learn to make your point, and then get on with the review and keep the copy moving— and cut, cut, cut. My first review on one major paper was done to precise specifications as to length; a more recent review had to be written to an exact number of *lines*, mind you, with the typewriter margins set at so-and-so. You're going to have to learn to enjoy cutting as much as you enjoy writing.

Kipling is a fine example of this. Writing his Indian stories, he says he learned that "a tale from which pieces have been raked out is like a fire that has been poked. One does not know that the operation has been performed, but everyone feels the effect."

As an editor, I admit to one prejudice. I want writers who give a damn—about writing, about the truth, about honest effort. This means, for one thing, that you must be ready to love the book you're reviewing if it gives you any chance to love it. If it doesn't, say so, by all means. If it's terrible, give it both barrels. But remember that your stance is not that of a hanging judge. It's that of a person passionately involved in reading matter, and impatient with any writer who isn't at least enough involved himself to give you a good honest piece of work to review.

The point is not to waste your deadliest shots on the mediocre book, or the book that tried but didn't make it. If there is something there to encourage, encourage it. Don't lean on the faults too hard, if the writer shows some signs of being improvable. And please—no *ad hominem* attacks.

My magazine, *BooksWest*, is a trade journal whose readership is largely made up of booksellers and librarians. This means that our reviews have slightly different responsibilities to meet from those of other journals. We have to consider not only the quality of the book but also the salability or utility of it. We are, in effect, ordering books for the bookseller, who has to be able to keep his customers happy and his doors open. We are advising librarians, too, and their problems are even more acute in some ways. The bookseller sometimes gets books on consignment, while the librarian is stuck with his order forever. And if, on our bad advice, the librarian orders only one copy of *Roots* (most libraries did, in fact, under-order that amazing book), or, on the other hand, orders 35 copies of *Better Beekeeping* for a small city branch library, he's in trouble, and we helped put him there. This knowledge should temper the subjective notions we put on paper when we review books, and if we let up on this we're being less than fair to our readers.

Librarians, in particular, have to have solidly authoritative reviews in the genres. *BooksWest*, thus, tends to assign category-fiction hardbacks—mysteries, science fiction, Gothics —to regular columnists with good names in their specialties. John Ball reviews mysteries, for instance, and A. J. Budrys reviews science fiction. You aren't totally out of the running here, though. By the time this appears in print, *BooksWest* will be the largest review market in America for that neglected stepchild of the publishing world, the $450-million mass-market paperback business.

BooksWest reviews not only paperback originals—an increasingly important part of the trade—but reprints as well. And we have no restrictions about re-reviewing a book we earlier covered in hardback. After all, the paperback customer is often a very different person from the hardback buyer, and he could use a fresh point of view. Feedback from booksellers indicates that you can stack the hardback and the paperback reprints right next to each other on the remainder table without affecting the sales pattern: the paperback people will often buy the paperback version even if the hardback right beside it is marked down, and is cheaper than the paperback reprint version.

What does this mean for us as reviewers? Only this: the paperback readers' attitudes are different from the hardback readers'. You can't impress anyone by leaving a paperback on the coffee table to be noticed. You can't show off fine bindings that way either. Paperback readers by and large read for pleasure, not for show (and good for them, too!), and they are likely to be a trifle more honest about their tastes and dislikes than hardback purchasers. We'd better keep that in mind and be honest with them ourselves.

In our paperback section, too, we are advising not only the reader who loves poetry and beautiful letters; we are also advising the lady who loves Gothics, historical romances, and Harlequin romances. And we're advising, by extension, the reader who can't get enough of Louis L'Amour, Nick Carter, or The Executioner. And we can't go writing down to any of them, or dispensing Culture from any Olympian height.

This means a number of things. In reviewing category novels, we have to know the basic attitudes underlying each. These must influence our reviewing approach. We must not review a good Gothic as if it were a failed attempt at Jane Austen, but must place it correctly among its natural, contemporary competitors. The Gothic formula is rigid, and to the novice it would appear full of clichés. We have to remember, though, that a plot device unacceptable in a "serious" novel might be quite acceptable in a Gothic. The same is true also of westerns, and the problem becomes really acute with science fiction, whose readers are highly sophisticated about their genre and often very vocal about this. We have to know what they want and advise them on the basis of up-to-date knowledge of their field.

Perhaps what I'm saying here is that in reviewing mass-market paperbacks our authority must be real, not assumed. We're dealing with people who really love these categories, and we must love them, too. There is something dishonest about taking the reader's dollar to review books in a category we do not, ever, visit for our own reading pleasure. No matter that this principle is flouted in certain other journals; we at *BooksWest* have strong feelings about this. We want reviewers who can approach a book with an open mind, at least now and then; we recently wrote of a Kay Thorpe romance, "Would you believe a Harlequin so well written that a man can enjoy it?"

That about wraps up our approach. If you're prejudiced against the "oater" because "women don't like westerns," you're going to miss some good reading (Lee Hoffman's fine novels, for instance, which appeal to both sexes equally). You're also going to turn off readers, who want their westerns reviewed by people who *like* a good western, and who care about the form.

Back at the beginning, I mentioned that you had first to get the chance to wear the reviewer's hat—and that's mainly a matter of being persistent and of keeping your eyes and ears open—and then you must get the reader to let you continue to wear it. Please the editor to get in the door; please the reader to stay there. This doesn't imply a lot of servile catering and pandering. What it does mean is staying honest, entertaining—an overlooked facet of the trade—and above all authoritative. You don't have to be a know-it-all polymath like Nero Wolfe. Nobody knows everything. But once you've begun to find that voice of yours, it mustn't falter under new influences. Remember, you're a professional writer (if you aren't, you're not ready; it's that simple).

That means you could, if the occasion demanded, be put in an empty room with nothing but a typewriter and a sheet or two of white paper, and in a certain length of time you could turn out one or two hundred readable, entertaining— and salable—words about virtually any subject, without so much as a pocket reference at your elbow. And, of course, the only voice you could use in a hat trick like that—the only voice that would work at all—would be the one you were born with, the one you have so painfully labored to find, and train, and feed, until it can, easily and fluently, say the only things you'll ever be cut out to say. That's all.

JAN FRAZER writes free-lance reviews on a regular basis for several Florida newspapers and a regional magazine. She also has a book review program on a local radio station there, as well as in Maine; gives televised reviews for a Florida cable TV channel; and lectures frequently on books and authors.

11 | Book Reviewing at the Local Level

by JAN FRAZER

WHEN MY youngest child reached nursery school age, I found myself with three hours, five days a week, that were totally mine. Before the arrival of the children, I had been a copywriter for seven years. My problem was, what could I write and complete in fifteen hours a week? I decided book reviews for the local weekly paper might be a good possibility.

I wrote a review of Ernest Hemingway's *Islands in the Stream* and took it to the editor of *The Naples* [Florida] *Star,* suggesting that I do a weekly review. She was hardly ecstatic about a book review feature but agreed to run a few to see whether they drew any reader response. When she received some enthusiastic mail about the reviews, I became a permanent free lancer for the paper for the next six years. I then switched my reviewing to the Sunday edition of *The Naples Daily News,* which has a larger circulation.

After four months of writing newspaper reviews, I persuaded the general manager of our local radio station to give my book review program a 13-week trial run. I've been broadcasting book reviews twice a week over WNOG ever since.

During the summer months, my husband's business used to take us all to Northeast Harbor, Maine. As soon as we arrived there, I got in touch with the station manager of WDEA in Ellsworth, Maine. He proved to be the easiest person of all to sell, because he was a reader. Then I found a local paper within the station's range to purchase the co-ordinated newspaper reviews.

My book review business continues to snowball. For several years I have televised my reviews over Cable-Vision Two, which serves southwest Florida. I now deliver lectures to area clubs and review a potpourri of nine to eleven books in a program. I have a book page, concerned with books of interest to Floridians, in a regional magazine.

I do not consider myself a book critic. If a book fails to interest me, or is poorly written, I don't review it. Basically, I think of myself as a "screening device," selecting from the more than 40,000 trade books published annually, fifty-two titles I think my readers, listeners, and viewers would enjoy. I use each review in my three media outlets. It is first published in the newspaper, a week later it is heard over radio, and a month later seen on television.

The radio reviews, which average three-and-a-half minutes each, are taped six at a time at WNOG. The tape is mailed to WDEA in Maine after it has run in Florida. The television reviews are video-taped twelve at a time and are shown twice a week.

The financial compensation is not very substantial, unless you count all the free review copies from publishers. The three separate broadcasting sponsors pay the stations for air time and include a talent fee for me. The newspapers, magazines and area clubs pay me directly.

It is rewarding to realize that you are influencing your area's reading habits. Local librarians tell me they get phone calls after each of my reviews from people who want to be put on the reserve list for the book reviewed that week. During the week I reviewed Peter Benchley's *Jaws,* thirty-five copies were sold in one bookstore alone.

For the free lancer with a limited amount of writing time, book reviewing at the local level can evolve into a satisfying mini-career. Most small-market media prefer to use a local reviewer rather than a "big name." Reviewing is also an excellent way to find out what kinds of books are accepted for publication.

How to get started . . .

1. Write three or four reviews as a test run for your local paper and if they are accepted, request a small supply of the newspaper's stationery as compensation. Use the stationery to request your first review copies from publishers.

2. Take out a subscription to the trade magazine of the publishing industry, *Publishers Weekly.* There is a section called "Forecasts" in *PW* which contains brief evaluations of soon-to-be-published books.

3. Get a copy of *Literary Market Place* (Bowker). *LMP* will provide you with publishers' addresses and the names of their publicity directors to whom you will write requesting books for review. After you have established yourself as a regular reviewer, request a listing in *LMP.* This will give you more credibility and make it easier to obtain review copies.

4. Always send two copies of your published review or

two copies of your radio-television script to the publisher. That is how you pay for your review copy. The publisher will keep one and send the other to the author. Some reviewers are careless about this and later wonder why they have trouble getting review copies.

5. Keep a pad and a pen at your side when you read a book for review. Jot down page numbers and brief notes on material you want to use in your review. Once you've finished the book, you'll need your notes and page numbers, so you won't waste time thumbing back and forth through the book to locate a description of the main character, or a particular passage you want to quote to illustrate the author's style.

6. Decide how you want to arrange the heading of your review by checking published reviews in newspapers and magazines. Once you get your heading set up, follow that style in all subsequent reviews. I have my newspaper review heading set in bold type in this style:

The Audubon Society Book of Wild Birds
By Les Line and Franklin Russell
Harry N. Abrams, Inc.
292 pages, 200 photos $35.00

When a book is illustrated, I like to show how many illustrations are included, because it helps justify the publisher's higher price.

7. Begin your review with a strong narrative hook to insure reader interest. Here are examples of opening paragraphs of four of my reviews:

What was Adolf Hitler? A fanatic, a genius, a mass murderer, a hypnotic orator, a gambler, a statesman? (*Adolf Hitler,* by John Toland)
Although on July 4, 1976, Los Angeles County claimed its

almost eleven-mile parade was the longest in the nation and in Washington, D.C. some thirty-three and a half tons of fireworks brightened up the sky, clearly the best place to have observed the Bicentennial was New York City. For it was only in New York that one could witness the greatest nautical event of the century—the silent, graceful progress of the Tall Ships up the Hudson River from the Verrazano Bridge to the George Washington Bridge. (*The Tall Ships,* by Hyla M. Clark)

In the early morning hours of February 19, 1969, the most glamorous socialite and renowned horsewoman in Houston, Texas, died at Sharpstown Hospital. Her name was—Joan Robinson Hill. She was 38 years old. (*Blood and Money,* by Thomas Thompson)

For centuries, viewers of Leonardo da Vinci's famous portrait of Mona Lisa have been intrigued by the enigmatic smile on her serene countenance and the knowing expression in her soft brown eyes that suggest she possesses a secret that will never be revealed. Pierre La Mure combed the archives of Florence, Milan, the Vatican and Paris to find answers to the questions that plagued him about the mysterious Mona Lisa. (*The Private Life of Mona Lisa,* by Pierre La Mure)

8. The nonfiction book is the easiest to review. You pick out facts that are new and interesting to you and paraphrase them. This gives the reader a sampling of what is in the book and may intrigue him enough to make him want to read it. At the very least, your review will have given the reader a few new thoughts for the day.

Here is my entire review of *The Audubon Society Book of Wild Birds*:

From the majestic pair of trumpeter swans winging across the dust jacket with the mist-shrouded, conifer-clad Alaskan mountains in the background, to the final unique photograph of an Australian lyrebird, this volume consistently maintains the highest degree of photographic excellence.

The more than two hundred full-color photographs were selected by the editors of *Audubon* magazine from literally thousands of transparencies taken by hundreds of professional photographers. Ten photographs taken by Naples resident Dr. M. Philip Kahl are included in the volume.

The informative text has been considerately set in extra-large type. Each of the fifteen chapters begins with an essay by Franklin Russell to introduce the particular group of birds and detail the environment in which they struggle to survive.

The writing is image-provoking, vivid and alive. For example, the section "Hunters in the Night" begins: "The somber yellow eyes perceive the victim, a snake, in the dim light. The great horned owl launches itself, tail raised, feet clenched to its belly. The owl is silent on outspread pinions and is aimed accurately, its body tilted backward as it approaches the snake, the pantalooned legs swinging forward in a perfect arc.

"The snake, rearing up in alarm, faces two sets of outspread, armored talons. It strikes but hits only reptile-like scales. In the next instant it is gripped by the talons. Desperately, the snake thrashes, coils its body around the owl's legs. The owl responds by fluffing out its feathers so greatly that the venomous fangs of the snake strike uselessly again and again at the feathers. Eventually the owl changes its grip, seizes the head of the snake and crushes it. The fight is over."

There's a wealth of information in this volume. When feeding, the black skimmer plows the water at a speed of twenty feet a second with the knife-like mandible immersed nearly to the mouth. We learn that the largest flying creature is the albatross which can attain a wingspan of eighteen feet enabling it to zigzag halfway around the world in a month. The albatross is so totally ocean-oriented that it may not see land for months or even years. Songbirds use their song as a communication tool. Their songs can warn of imminent danger, signal migration time and indicate their readiness to breed.

The grace, the beauty, and the perfection of *The Audubon Society Book of Wild Birds* is a constant delight. We see a large colony of three-foot-tall king penguins nesting on a sub-antarctic island and learn from Les Line's informative caption that "the single egg is carried on the feet of the male, protected from the cold by a warm fold of belly skin and feathers where the temperature is kept between 99° to 101° F."

The bright plumage of the jungle birds appears jewel-like against the dark, dense background of the Amazonian jungle: the dazzling ruby-red Brazilian tanager, the glistening emerald-green tanager and the brilliant sapphire-blue hyacinth macaw.

Les Line, editor of *Audubon* magazine, is the author of *The Sea Has Wings* and *Seasons,* as well as the editor of two Audubon anthologies, *This Good Earth* and *The Pleasure of Birds.*

Franklin Russell is the author of numerous magazine articles and more than a dozen books, including *Season on the Plain, Argen the Gull,* and *Watchers at the Pond.*

In the opening paragraph of the above review, I wanted image-provoking phrases that would stimulate the reader to see in his mind's eye the exceptional photographs.

The job of the second paragraph was to let the reader know the photographs were selected by experts and, of interest to the Naples community, was the fact that ten were taken by a Neopolitan.

The third paragraph explains, in general, how the book is set up. The fourth and fifth paragraphs deal with the excellent writing style and include a fairly lengthy quote as proof.

Paragraphs six, seven, and eight contain those interesting facts paraphrased. The final two paragraphs give the editors' backgrounds and previous credits.

9. The most difficult books to review are mysteries, psychological thrillers, and espionage-suspense novels, because you can only reveal the very beginning of the complex plots. You must concern yourself mainly with the characters, the

setting, and the author's background. Here is my review of *The Man Who Wasn't There*, by Roderick MacLeish:

The human mind is a fragile thing and Rod MacLeish proves in his ingeniously plotted, pychological thriller just what a shaky hold one man has on his sanity.

The central question in the story is, can an individual be deliberately driven completely mad to the point where he will commit an act totally foreign to his nature?

The choreographer of this journey into madness is Edouard Fouier, the French psychiatrist, infamous for his experiments in primal madness. Given a detailed description of a man's entire life experience—his fears, his habits, his fragilities and hangups, Fouier knows he can drive that person mad. He's been successful with this experiment on two previous occasions.

It is unnecessary for Fouier to meet his subject-victim. The entire process can be conducted from his shabby flat in Paris through a messenger who will relay Fouier's instructions to those close to the victim and report back with the results of his psychological manipulations. Fouier will be paid one hundred thousand dollars for his work.

The marionette whose psychological strings are being pulled in this dreadful dance toward madness is Rex Carnaby, the American movie star.

Numb with exhaustion, Rex is in a vulnerable state. In the past five days, he has completed his most demanding role in a film and buried his mother. His attempts to contact his half-sister Maggie in time for the funeral ended in failure.

On his flight home to Washington, Rex innocently indulges in a game he often plays when a celebrity hunter corners him. He tells his seatmate Harry Follensbee that he is not Rex Carnaby, but his twin brother, Frederick Jackson Carnaby. After drawing Follensbee out in conversation to learn his areas of knowledge, Rex chooses a career for the non-existent Fred. He decides to be an animal importer, operating out of Kenya, selling wild animals to zoos all over the world. Rex invents great tales of

African adventure to pass the time and escape from reality. When they part at Dulles Airport, Rex tells Follensbee he's off to London after a day's visit with his sister, then home to Kenya.

Two days later, Rex stares in disbelief at a picture of himself on the obituary page of *The New York Times*. The headline reads, "Frederick Jackson Carnaby, Animal Dealer, Twin of Actor, Dies En Route to London." Fouier's third experiment in primal madness has begun.

Rod MacLeish is a senior commentator for the Westinghouse Broadcasting Company and a columnist for the *Washington Post*. His previous books include *A Time of Fear* (a novel); *The Sun Stood Still* (about Arab-Israeli relations); *The Guilty Bystander* (a collection of his broadcast commentaries) and *A City on the River* (a political study of Washington). He is currently at work on a new novel, *Orlov's Daughter,* which falls into the espionage-suspense category.

The nephew of poet Archibald MacLeish, Rod MacLeish is the son of the late Norman MacLeish, the American artist who was a Naples winter resident for many years.

10. Try for a conversational style, rhythm in your phrasing, uncommon words and vivid images to help you express your ideas in a way that will reach your audience. When you find yourself displeased with what you've written and keep changing words that don't seem to satisfy you or convey what you have in mind, put it away and come back to it fresh the next morning. You'll find the review will practically revise itself.

11. Use your family and friends as sounding boards. Tell them about a new book you've finished reading and watch their faces for the interest spark as you tell them about it.

12. Never use a book as a springboard for an elaborate personal essay on a subject close to your heart. Your review should be about the book, so the reader can determine whether or not it is a book he wants to read.

13. Be sure you make a "value judgment" of the book at some point. Is the author's writing style exceptionally good? Are the characters well-rounded, the plot believable? How is suspense handled? If it's history or biography, was the subject extensively researched? Compare it to other books in the same genre. If the book has minor flaws, point them out. Decide whether the author accomplished what he set out to do. How will the reader benefit from the book? Will it entertain him? Increase his knowledge in a particular field? Provide escape reading from our world of future shock?

14. Give the author's background, mentioning previously published works. If the movie rights to the book have been sold or it is a book club selection, include that information.

15. If you don't feel you have the voice or diction to broadcast and televise your reviews, don't let that stop you. If you can sell your local station on the idea of carrying your weekly book review, a member of the broadcasting staff can deliver it. My radio and television reviews are essentially the same as the newspaper reviews, but usually do not include as much of the author's background, because of the three-and-a-half-minute time limit. My radio reviews are broadcast during what the stations call "drive time" when people are driving to or from their jobs. Of all my media reviews, the ones on radio probably reach the largest audience.

16. Make a point of varying the types of books you review, so your reviews are of particular interest to different segments of your audience. One week, review a best seller everyone's talking about, the next week, a how-to book that will benefit the reader, and the following week a good Gothic novel that will provide an escape for the romantic.

ETHEL L. HEINS is Editor of *The Horn Book Magazine*. She has been a children's and school librarian and has served on several committees of the American Library Association, such as the Mildred L. Batchelder Award Committee and the Newbery and Caldecott Awards Committee, and has been a judge of children's books for the National Book Award. She is currently a faculty member of the Simmons College Center for the Study of Children's Literature.

12

Some Problems and Perils in Children's Book Reviewing

by ETHEL L. HEINS

IT IS only when we acknowledge that children's books are a legitimate part of universal literature—and not a negligible subgenre—that we can discuss the reviewing and criticism of literature for children. And it is almost axiomatic that a deep and underlying respect for both books and children should direct, inspire, and focus the reviewing of children's books.

Thousands of words have been written on the difference between reviewing and criticism, but it is still important to set down some wisely enunciated opinions. In "Reviewing," her famous essay written in 1939, Virginia Woolf put it squarely: "The critic is separate from the reviewer; the function of the reviewer is partly to sort current literature; partly to advertise the author; partly to inform the public." What is the essential difference between book reviewing and genuine criticism? Is literary criticism involved in book reviewing? Journalistic reviewing is mainly concerned with the present; it attempts to relate the book to an immediate audience, especially to people who have not read the book. And since its purpose is advisory, it can be regarded as a utilitarian service. But perhaps we should remember that Virginia Woolf also remarked, "It is a matter of the very greatest interest to a writer to know what an honest and intelligent reader thinks about his work." To which her husband, Leonard Woolf, added his own opinion on the function of a review: "It is to give to readers a description of the book and an estimate of its quality in order that he may know whether or not it is the kind of book which he may want to read. Reviewing is therefore quite distinct from literary criticism."

In a London *Times Literary Supplement* essay, Graham Hough of Cambridge University injected a note of humility into the whole discussion: "Criticism is either the secondary occupation of imaginative writers, or it is the occupation of the middlemen of literature—scholars, teachers, and journalists. Literature has need of its middlemen, but they are the diffusers and transmitters of culture, not its creators." The critic must bear in mind that he is less important than the artist. True criticism, of course, probes beyond the immediate; it should be timeless rather than ephemeral, and some criticism—like Aristotle's, which has lasted for more than two thousand years—has itself become literature.

Many people who judge children's books are convinced that criticism and reviewing often coincide, that they combine the best of both worlds when their evaluations constitute *critical* reviews. Most journals and newspapers cover only a fraction of the children's books published annually. Thus the reviewer's very act of selection can constitute an exercise in criticism. The time-honored process begins with the questions: What was the author's intention—what did he or she try to accomplish? And the next question must, inevitably, be: How well has the author succeeded? Furthermore, in dealing with books for children, still another question can be posed: How appropriate is the result? The answers are not simple, for literary evaluation—and its important adjuncts, analogies and comparisons—requires a body of knowledge and critical skill.

Since children's books generally do not receive the extended critical treatment in various media that adult books do, the reviews of them frequently tend to be descriptive and commendatory. Even *The Horn Book Magazine*, which is entirely concerned with books for young people, has space limitations and publishes all too few negative reviews. This situation is not entirely deplorable. No less a critic than John Dryden once said, "They wholly mistake the nature of criticism who think its business is principally to find fault. Criticism, as it was first instituted by Aristotle, was meant a standard of judging well; the chiefest part of which is, to observe those excellencies which should delight a reasonable reader." Of course, there are always people who believe that the more censorious you are, the more scorn you heap upon a book, the more perceptive a critic you must be. But certain books merit—or fairly demand—strong unfavorable statements, particularly if the author has previously produced some highly acclaimed work. In fact, one publisher freely said, "When an opinion is unfavorable, it may cause distress to the publisher and anguish to the author, but unless it is demonstrably unfair, prejudiced, or inaccurate, publishers and experienced authors swallow their disappointment. . . . What other business welcomes, even invites, criticism of its products, knowing that the rough must be taken with the smooth?"

Children's book reviewers should be chosen for their knowledge of both children's literature and general literature, their knowledge of childhood and a lifeline of communication with children, taste and judgment in the field of aesthetics, critical acumen, and the ability to express themselves without prejudice or pomposity in clear, intelligent, unhackneyed prose. It is the reviewer's consolation to rejoice in what delights him or her and to deplore what disappoints, although many years must pass, according to Matthew Arnold, before one can deliver an opinion that is not "only personal, but personal with passion."

Special problems

Now if children's literature can justifiably be considered a part of general literature, why should the reviewing of it be different? For it *is* different. Reviews of books for adults are read by adults: the reviewer is writing for the potential reader of the book. But no matter how bookish a child may be, he rarely, if ever, reads reviews of children's books—which are, of course, written for adults. As Paul Heins wrote in *The Horn Book*, "Children's literature . . . is not the concern of children alone. Parents, teachers, and librarians as well as authors, illustrators, and publishers are potential judges of books for children . . . [As a result] the reviewing and criticism of children's literature is more complex and fraught with misconceptions than any other kind of reviewing and criticism." The same criteria must apply to books for children as to those for adults; but since pragmatism, and not a consuming interest in the books themselves, is so often the motive behind both the reviewing and the reading of the reviews, the well-known standards tend to grow somewhat fuzzy. It may be helpful to point out to the unwary some of the problems peculiar to the reviewing of children's books.

1. Recognition of the fact that one of the joys of reading is personal discovery should discourage precise age or personality tagging of children's books. Thus, broad rather than specific age groupings should be suggested, and especially hazardous are such statements as "a *must* for every library" or "a book of certain appeal for all little girls" or "every child who has ever longed for a pony will identify with the hero of this book."

2. All books can be reviewed from several nonliterary points of view; the tortured psychoanalytical perspective on children's books is scarcely new. In 1963, Frederick C. Crews published his magnificent spoof on literary criticism, *The Pooh Perplex* (Dutton). In the chapter called "Poisoned Paradise: The Underside of *Pooh*," the critic writes: "We have the rationale of the ideal world that Christopher Robin has hallucinated—a pastoral paradise, a garden of fun in which the danger of incest and punishment is nil. But like all such gardens . . . something is likely to go awry sooner or later. In this case it is the entrance of Kanga that transforms *Winnie-the-Pooh*, with one brutal stroke, from the genre of bucolic idyll to that of depth-psychological tale of terror." As everyone knows, this was written by a sophisticated professor as a huge joke; but only last year the review of a slightly zany but perfectly innocent picture book accused the artist of filling her book with phallic symbols!

3. Another nonliterary view is what is now called "the issues approach" or "the message approach" to children's literature. Most books have an underlying idea or a discernible theme; but the *theme* of a book should not be confused with a *message*; and it is a cruel and futile misuse of litera-

ture to employ the tactics of vigilantes to track down messages in children's books. One cannot disagree that books
can be powerful instruments for moral and intellectual
growth and the development of social awareness. But a whole
school of witch-hunting has developed: well-meaning teachers, journalists, and sociologists who view books from oblique
angles and whose judgments are laced with didacticism. It is
the reviewer's right—even obligation—to assess and illuminate a book; it is not the critic's job, however, to tell the
author what the plot should have included or how the
characters should have behaved. The adult's temptation to
instruct is irresistible, but a work of art is not a political or
a social tract nor should its purpose be rhetorical persuasion
or moral improvement. For authors cannot assume the roles
of teacher, mentor, preacher; they are artists, and books
viewed as tools cease to exist in their own right and become
simply the raw material from which lessons are hammered
out.

4. Children's books have naturally been affected by the
same revolutionary social and moral upheavals that have left
their mark on all other aspects of modern life. Books cast in
untraditional molds or dealing with new and urgent subject
matter have caused many reviewers to widen their horizons.
On the other hand, it would be easy to be swept overboard by
the strong winds of change. Reviewers must still evaluate
books first of all on literary and artistic merit; they should
neither accept nor reject a book simply because of its theme
or subject matter. And although in a society as diverse as
ours it would be unfair to place disproportionate emphasis
on everything in a book which could conceivably offend
someone, reviewers occasionally are obliged to refer to obviously controversial elements to make the purchaser aware of
his own responsibility.

5. It is not the function of the reviewer to express concern about the popularity of a book, although an adult book selector may need or wish to take this into consideration. It would be unthinkable for the reviewer of a book for adults to make such an impertinent statement as: "A brilliant achievement but, unfortunately, not destined to be popular with the average reader." The serious critic has good reason to worry about the implications of judging children's books by childish standards. On the other hand, reviewers must remain aware that they are appraising *children's* books—even though at this juncture the statement may seem paradoxical. You have often heard an author claim, "Oh, but I don't write for children; I write to please myself." Perhaps this protest stems from a contemptuous attitude toward children's books; surely the author must realize the importance of a sense of audience. John Rowe Townsend, both an author and a critic, has come to terms with the apparent contradiction: "If the book is for children he should not let his mind be dominated by the fact; but neither, I think, should he attempt to ignore it . . . Just as the author must, I believe, write for himself yet with an awareness of an audience of children, so the critic must write for himself with an awareness that the books he discusses are books written for children."

Guiding principles

So far I have presented a case for the literary criticism of children's books—with a few admonitions. But novice reviewers need not only principles but a few useful precepts as well.

Of all books, fiction presents the greatest challenge; the distinctive and the trivial are easily recognized, while the merely mediocre often throws an inexperienced reviewer into an agony of doubt. Consideration must be given to originality and imagination, style and structure, emotional depth, and verisimilitude in the re-creation of time, place, and setting. Are characterizations full-bodied, is the plot handled skillfully enough to create tension—and how effective is the language, the author's power of expression? Important, too, is the suitability of the style to the book—encompassing everything from the terse, humorous, simple storytelling of Beverly Cleary, who has an uncanny ability to echo the natural thoughts and conversation of children, to the mature artistry and subtlety of the writing of Virginia Hamilton.

Fantasy must meet all the requirements of fiction; but while it offers the writer added dimensions, it demands an even greater degree of creative imagination than so-called realistic fiction. Transcending clever invention or mere flights of fancy, successful fantasy must induce in the reader Coleridge's "willing suspension of disbelief" by creating reality out of illusion.

Historical fiction, too, has its own special criteria. It should not only present events out of the past but it should confront the young reader with the significance of the past. Archaic language and costumed figures do not provide credibility. So steeped must the writer be in the history of his chosen period that he will be able to evoke an unmistakable atmosphere and breathe life into his characters, who are wholly affected by the time and place.

The ramifications of picture books are so numerous and complex that the subject cannot be dealt with briefly. A picture book is a work in which the text is sparse and the story or idea is presented partly through illustrations. Words and images should be integrated, mutually dependent and worthy of each other; whether or not the author is also the artist, there must be an underlying unity. Pictures not only share the storytelling; they illuminate, interpret, and sometimes elaborate the text, revealing subtleties of character, mood, action, and setting. With highly developed technical resources available for the faithful reproduction of art, a picture book can be a totally individual creation, unique in subject, treatment, graphic style, design, size, shape, and typography. But the young child's approach to the book is not an aesthetic one; he is unaware of style, technique, and composition, nor is he fascinated by sheer brilliant, pretentious artwork or by clever adult humor. And it is essential that silly exaggeration and sentimentality do not substitute for genuine humor and emotion.

The range of nonfiction is as seemingly endless as the curiosities and interests of childhood, and the varieties of imaginative format for differing levels of age and sophistication are equally limitless. The basic volume on children's nonfiction is Margery Fisher's *Matters of Fact* (Crowell); but a few salient points and questions may be indicated here. Factual material should be accurate, authoritative, up-to-date, objectively presented, conveniently and logically arranged. An adequate table of contents and a generous index make the information accessible. Illustrations, whether they are drawings or photographs, should be pertinent, clear, and realistic; the literary style should be lucid and fluent. One can ask: Is the presentation suited to the intended audience? Is it simple enough—or ridiculously oversimplified? And what are the author's qualifications? American publishers can well take pride in a sizable body of superb nonfiction produced for children.

One can find few critics of children's books more appreciative or demanding than Lillian H. Smith. In her book, *The Unreluctant Years* (A.L.A.), she writes: "The ability to distinguish a good book from a poor one, to know when the spirit of literature is present and when it is not, requires the sensitive feeling and reasoning of the reader. . . . There is no formula we can apply which will infallibly tell us whether what we are reading is good or bad. Familiarity with and understanding of the books which have been proved to have permanent value will give a bedrock of reasoning and feeling which one can work from, and go back to, in the evaluating of contemporary writing for children."

L. E. Sissman was contributing editor and columnist for *The Atlantic*, where his monthly column,
"Innocent Bystander," appeared monthly. He
wrote book reviews regularly for *The New
Yorker*, which also published his poetry frequently.

13

Reviewer's Dues
by L. E. Sissman

After years of stumping and (I hoped) dazzling other
people with anything I cared to try in verse, at the hoary
age of forty I became a book reviewer. Now it was my sworn
and bounden duty to penetrate and unravel the obscurities of
other writers' methods and messages, to dissipate the wet
and inky smokescreen in which the wily squid conceals himself, and to set the delicate skeleton of the author's true
design in so many words before my readers. Besides being
hard, grueling detective work, this was both scary and risky;
armed only with a shaky analytic gift and my spotty, idiosyncratic store of reading, I was laying my sacred honor
on the line each time I tried to pick another literary lock
in public.

For the first couple of years, I drove myself to write reviews like an aristocrat driving himself to the gallows, with
superficial sangfroid as thin as onionskin and a real clutch
of fear each time I sat down at the typewriter.

Then, mercifully, I began to learn the ropes and look a

little more objectively around me. I discovered that reviewing was not simply something that a *soi-disant* literary man did to fill time, amplify his tiny reputation, and (of course) earn a little money. *Au contraire.* Reviewing, it was slowly and astoundingly revealed to me, was a vocation, a craft, a difficult discipline, with its own rules and customs, with a set of commandments and a rigid protocol. Mostly by making painful mistakes and leaping brashly into pitfalls, I began to amass some notion of the shape of a reviewer's obligations to himself, to the author he reviews, to his editor, to his readers.

In short, I became aware of the moral imperatives of book reviewing. Funny as that may sound in a literary world raddled by cliques and claques and politics, by backscratching and back-stabbing, by overpraise and undernotice, I now believe that the would-be conscientious reviewer must be guided by a long list of stern prohibitions if he is to keep faith with himself and his various consumers. In the interests of controversy (and, I hope, of air-clearing), I set these down herewith.

1. Never review the work of a friend. All sorts of disasters are implicit here; a man and his work should be separate in the reviewer's mind, and the work should be his only subject. If you know the man at all well, you become confused and diffident; your praise becomes fulsome, and you fail to convey the real merits and demerits of the book to the poor reader. The hardest review I ever wrote was of the (quite good) novel of a friend four years ago. Never again.

2. Never review the work of an enemy. Unless you fancy yourself as a public assassin, a sort of licensed literary hit man, you will instinctively avoid this poisonous practice like

the plague it is. Corollary: never consent to be a hatchet man. If Editor X knows you are an old enemy of Novelist Y, he may (and shame on him, but it happens all the time) call on you to review Y's latest book. Beware, on pain of losing your credibility.

3. Never review a book in a field you don't know or care about. Once or twice I've been touted onto titles far from my beaten track. The resulting reviews were teeth-grindingly difficult to write and rotten in the bargain. Unless you're a regular polymath, stick to your own last.

4. Never climb on bandwagons. You are not being paid to subscribe to a consensus, nor will your reader thank you for it. If a book has been generally praised (or damned), you add nothing to anybody's understanding by praising (or damning) it in the same terms. Only if you have read the book with care and found something fresh to comment on should you attempt a review. Otherwise, find something else (how about the work of an unknown?) to write about. Or skip it; you'll earn that money you need for a new 500mm mirror lens somewhere else.

5. Never read other reviews before you write your own. This is a tough rule to follow, because all reviewers are naturally curious about the reception of Z's latest book. Nonetheless, you can't help being subtly influenced by what *The New York Times* reviewer (or whoever) has to say. Eschew!

6. Never read the jacket copy or the publisher's handout before reading and reviewing a book. Jacket copy (I know; I used to write it) is almost invariably misleading and inaccurate. The poor (literally: these downtrodden souls are, along with retail copywriters, the most underpaid people in advertising) writer is probably working from a summary

compiled by the sales department, not from a firsthand
reading of the book. The handouts are more of the same,
only flackier.

7. Never review a book you haven't read at least once.
Believe it or not, some reviewers merely skim a book (or
even depend on, horrors, the jacket copy) before reviewing
it. Not only is this a flagrant abdication of responsibility;
there is always the lurking danger of missing a vital clue in
the text and making a public spectacle of yourself. It should
happen frequently to all such lazy reviewers.

8. Never review a book you haven't understood. If *you*
haven't figured out what the author is up to, there's simply
no way you can convey it to your reader. Reread the book;
if necessary, read some of the author's other books; if you
still don't know, forget it. The cardinal sin here is to go
right ahead and condemn a half-understood book on the
covert grounds that you haven't found its combination.

9. Never review your own ideas instead of the author's.
Unless you're the ranking pundit in the field and you have
a scholarly bone to pick with the author, you have no right
to use the book under inspection as a springboard for a
trumpet voluntary of your own.

10. Never fail to give the reader a judgment and a recom-
mendation on the book. And tell why. A reviewer is really a
humble consumer adviser; his main job is to tell the public
what to read and what to skip. It's an important job because
nobody can possibly keep up with all the books being published today.

11. Never neglect new writers. First novelists, in particular, get passed over too frequently for several reasons.
The obvious reason is that Norman Mailer's new novel is
better copy than Hannah Furlong's maiden effort. The less
obvious reason is that it's much harder for a reviewer to get

an intelligent fix on an unknown. In short, it's harder work to review a debutant.

12. Never assume that a writer is predictable. This is, in a way, the converse of the previous proposition. Part of the pleasure of picking up a new book by a writer you've read before is *knowing* what you're about to read—the themes, the style, the old, familiar tricks. But what if the novelist has *grown*; what if he does something daring and unexpected? That's when a lot of reviewers, myself included, are tempted to put him down for not rewriting himself. The only answer is to approach the book with great caution and read it on its own merits, forgetting what has gone before.

13. Never forget to summarize the story or the argument. What's more maddening than a review that rhapsodizes (or bitches) for two thousand words about the author's style, his technique, his place in letters without ever giving us a clue to the nature of the story, beyond the mention of an incident or two?

14. Never, on the other hand, write a review that is merely a plot summary and nothing more. This happens surprisingly often, especially in newspaper reviews. The reader of the review deserves a judgment, a rating, not simply a recapitulation.

15. Never impale a serious writer on his minor errors. Nobody's perfect, as the old gag line says, and, given the susceptibility of even the most powerful piece of work to ridicule, it is frighteningly easy for the reviewer to have his fun at the author's expense and end up distorting the value and import of the book. (Example: I recently read a good novel in which the author consistently misused the word "fulsome" and mixed up "she" and "her." It would have been an act of willful irresponsibility to take the author to task for these small miscues, which were also his editor's fault.)

16. Never write critical jargon. The day of the New Criticism, for all its merits, is mercifully past, and so, I'd hope, is the compulsion of some reviewers to pose and posture as anointed gospelers of the true and beautiful. The reviewer who writes for a general-circulation newspaper or magazine should have his typewriter unplugged if he persists in pedagogeries.

17. Never fail to take chances in judgment. Because it forces you to enter the mind of another on his own terms, reviewing is literally mind-expanding. Often the reviewer is astonished at his new conclusions and afraid to put them down on paper. This is a mistake; one of the highest critical acts is to arrive at a new understanding and communicate it to the reader.

18. Never pick a barn-door target to jeer at. Not long ago, one of the daily reviewers in *The New York Times* wasted an entire column on the new novel by one of the Irving Wallaces. Irving Stone? Jacqueline Susann? Or whoever. Anyway, it was painfully easy—shooting fish in a barrel— and painfully unworthy of the reviewer's taste and talent. He might far better have reviewed a good first novel.

19. Never play the shark among little fishes. Being a reviewer does not entitle you to savage the beginner, the fumbler, the less-than-accomplished writer. A sincere and decent effort demands a sincere and decent response. If you've ever struggled to write a book yourself, you know the vast amounts of pain and love it takes. To put down an honest attempt in gloating arrogance is to deal a crippling blow to a nascent career of possible promise.

20. Never compete with your subject. A reviewer is not, at least during his hours as a reviewer, a rival of the person he's reviewing. If he sees flaws in the work under inspection, he should report them, but he should not give vent to a long

harangue on how *he* would have written the book. (If his hubris is that keen, perhaps he should take time off and write a book himself.)

In a word, then, the sins and temptations of reviewers are legion. As an incumbent sinner, I have more often than I like to think about been brought up short by the realization of my own weaknesses. Thus the list above. While I know I don't have the constancy and fortitude to follow it to the letter, I try to bear it in mind, like a catechism, when I sit down to write about another person's work. It is the least I can do for another poor sufferer who has taken the supreme risk of letting his dreams and talents go forth between covers, and for all those poor sufferers who simply like to read, and who rely, for better or worse, on the dim and uncertain skills of reviewers for a guide through the maze of new titles in their bright, unrevealing jackets on the shelves.

Jon L. Breen contributes two regular mystery review columns: "The Jury Box," monthly in *Ellery Queen's Mystery Magazine,* and "The World of Mysteries Plus," six times a year in *Wilson Library Bulletin.* He is also the author of over 30 short stories for *EQMM* and *Alfred Hitchcock's Mystery Magazine* and has contributed articles to *The Armchair Detective, The New Republic, The Thoroughbred Record,* and other publications.

14

Reviewing Mysteries
by Jon L. Breen

I WRITE two regular columns covering the wide field of crime-mystery-suspense-detective fiction: "The Jury Box," monthly in *Ellery Queen's Mystery Magazine,* and "The World of Mysteries Plus," bimonthly in *Wilson Library Bulletin.* In both of these regular features, the selection of what I will write about is up to me. Ideally, I would read every new book published in the field and review the most noteworthy. Unfortunately, I don't read that fast, so my first problem is choosing what to read for review.

Some major writers are so important to the field that their new books are required reading for the reviewer—names like Ross Macdonald, Eric Ambler, Stanley Ellin, Julian Symons, P. D. James, and Emma Lathen. Another group is made up of books that attract me as a reader, either because the plot or background sounds intriguing or because they are by favorite authors. Any book with a serial killer, a locked room, a theatrical or sports background, or any new book by Bill Pronzini, Peter Lovesey, Joe Gores, or Robert Bloch, I will read because I can't stand not to. With the compulsory and the compulsive out of the way, I try to strike a balance among types of books. Ideally, each column in *EQMM* should include a new Gothic, a new spy story, a new pure detective story, something to satisfy the special tastes of every reader.

A promising-looking book by a new or unfamiliar writer should usually get the call over the latest by an established writer who produces a fairly consistent product. I assume a reader would rather be told that a talented newcomer's first novel is a winner than that the latest Inspector Smythe novel is up to (or down to) the usual standard.

Many crime novels and even some pure mystery novels are now being published and promoted as "mainstream" novels rather than as mysteries. Most of the "blockbuster" political and disaster novels qualify as mysteries—or anyway suspense—and recent years have seen several crime fiction experiments by mainstream writers. I like to include such in my columns whenever possible, but when it comes down to a choice, the "regular" mystery should have my first call for a couple of reasons. The blockbuster and mainstream novels are more likely to be reviewed elsewhere, and the regular mystery is likely to be a better one. It's too bad these artificial distinctions among types of writing exist, but since they do, the specialist reviewer has to be guided by them to some degree.

Given a large field like mystery or science fiction to cover, it is not a bad idea to use a few close friends or relatives whose judgment you trust as screeners. I rely on my wife to spot and pass along the best Gothics, and I give occasionally spy and adventure novels to my father for recommendations.

Though any reader will prefer one type of story over another, a good mystery reviewer must be able to appreciate a good job in any of the various sub-genres: classic puzzles, private-eye adventures, big capers, police procedurals, Gothics, espionage, Mafia stories, psychological suspense, occult, and the countless combinations of the above categories. My own bias is for the pure classic detective novel, and if more writers were doing books in the vein of Agatha Christie, John Dickson Carr, and Ellery Queen, nothing could make me happier. Gothics, on the other hand, would rate near the bottom of my personal preference list, but I can appreciate a good one. The Mafia story is the only type I have trouble enjoying, even when well done; to me professional, organized crime is the dullest possible subject for fiction, and I was able to lay *The Godfather* aside after 100 pages without a twinge, though not denying Puzo's storytelling skill.

Most of my reviews are of necessity extremely short, and it is a challenge to get enough information about a book into a small space. Though mystery novels are not devoid of allegory, symbolism, and thematic concerns, these factors are not generally what the writer is concentrating on or the reader is looking for.

There are four main elements to a good mystery: plot, pace, style, and characterization. A first-rate mystery novel should be strong in all four elements, though a number of writers (Erle Stanley Gardner is a prime example) have been adept enough in the first two to cancel out glaring deficiencies in the second two. Probably most writers in the mystery field are strongest on plot and weakest on style, while among "literary" writers, the reverse applies. The ideal review should touch on all four elements or, if brevity demands, tell which element is in the forefront.

When many titles must be covered briefly, a rating system can be helpful to differentiate quality. In "The Jury Box" column in *EQMM*, I use a system of from one to five stars to rate new novels and short story collections. Five stars indicates a potential classic and a candidate for inclusion in future "best" of the form. This rating appears very rarely. Four stars indicates a very good book, three stars a good one, two stars a book with deficiences in some area but some redeeming points, and one star an unredeemed failure. The one-star rating never appears, because to list one-star books would be to waste space.

The main pitfall of inexperienced mystery reviewers is spending too much space on plot summary. An unusual background or a particularly striking initial situation should be noted in the review, but extensive plot summary doesn't tell the reader anything about the quality of execution and frequently reveals too much for maximum enjoyment. (Publishers' blurbs do this even more frequently than reviews.)

The first rule of mystery reviewing seems at first glance too obvious even to need stating: You don't give away the ending. But it is still broken occasionally, usually (but not always) when mysteries have fallen into the hands of nonspecialist fiction reviewers. Almost all the reviewers of Ira Levin's *The Stepford Wives* gave away the book's secret in the course of their notices, performing a disservice to Levin and his potential readers. Irving Wallace's *The Seven Minutes*, essentially a mystery though not published as such, met a similar fate in the reviews.

Mystery reviewers know better but are not completely clean-handed in this regard. I didn't read Rex Stout's last Nero Wolfe novel, *A Family Affair*, until about a year after its first appearance and had, thus, read several reviews of it first. While none of the reviewers came right out and said who the murderer was, they dropped enough hints so that I picked up the book positive I knew who the murderer would be—and I was right.

Discussions of the endings are permissible in critical analyses of mystery novels when revealing the ending is necessary to make a particular point. When this is done, however, clear advance warning should be given, and such critical studies should be published long enough after the publication of the work in question to assume an audience who have read the book.

A reviewer or prospective reviewer of crime fiction, besides reading as many books in the field as possible, should also read as many reviews as possible. Though many newspapers and national magazines review mysteries on a regular basis, many of the best reviews of new mystery fiction appear in the amateur and semi-pro fan journals devoted to the field, most notably *The Armchair Detective*, whose reviewers often display a far deeper knowledge of the mystery field than the most prestigious national reviewers. The very *best* thing to do to study first-class mystery reviewing is to look through the back files of *The New York Times Book Review* between 1951 and 1967 for the work of the late Anthony Boucher, the finest reviewer the field has ever seen.

All reviewers, like all writers, have their peculiarities, and some of my habits I would not necessarily recommend to a newcomer entering the field. Like a sportswriter covering a ball game and writing a new lead for his story at the end of every inning, I often will write a review a sentence or two long when I'm midway through a novel and then read the rest of the book to see if my review holds up. Sometimes I have to change it, but often not.

I am usually reading several books at a time—one at home, one at work during breaks and lunch hour, and another (a paperback) to carry around and read at odd moments during the day. To do my job properly, I should read at least twenty or so books a month. (When selecting a suit or sports jacket, I must be sure a paperback book will fit in the inside pocket.)

Of course, when reading three books at once, I must be sure they are not too similar. Three snowed-in English house parties going at once will lead to inevitable confusion. Better it should be a Ngaio Marsh at home, an Ed McBain at work, and a Donald Hamilton in the pocket. Little chance of confusion there.

In a review column covering several books, it helps to be able to consider two or three together, and link them by a unifying paragraph introducing the column. The opening of this "Jury Box" column in one issue of *Ellery Queen's Mystery Magazine* provides an example:

Though theaters have long been a favorite locale for fictional murder, actor-detectives have been relatively few. Glyn Carr's mountain-climbing Sir Abercrombie Lewker, Carolyn Wells' retired movie idol Kenneth Carlisle, and Barnaby Ross' (Ellery Queen's) incomparable Drury Lane are three that come to mind.

At least two current series in the classic tradition feature thespian-sleuths. Simon Brett's *So Much Blood* (Scribners, $6.95) finds middle-aged actor Charles Paris presenting his one-man show on Thomas Hood on the fringes of the Edinburgh Festival while looking into the murder of another actor. The careful plotting, witty narration, and pointed satire of the British theatrical scene are up to the high standard set in Brett's first mystery, and the character of Paris grows in sympathy and complexity. (****)

Anne Morice's Tessa Crichton is the actress-wife of a Scotland Yard detective, but he is offstage in *Murder in Mimicry* (St. Martin's, $7.95). Tessa is in Washington, D.C. for a pre-

Broadway engagement of the latest British hit when the inevitable murder strikes the company. A solid conventional whodunit, soundly constructed and colorfully cast. (***)

The more customary outsider's viewpoint of actors and their foibles appears in H. R. F. Keating's *Filmi, Filmi, Inspector Ghote* (Doubleday Crime Club, $5.95). Murder comes to "Bollywood," the Indian film colony, as the star of a new version of Macbeth is killed by a fallen light, and Ghote (who must someday be played by Peter Sellers) finds the killer in his usual stumbling but determined manner. (***)

While the backgrounds of the three novels are noted, very little plot detail is given, though the unusual murder method in Keating's book is pointed out. The Brett novel, indicated by the four-star rating to be the best of the three, is praised for its plot, style, and characterization. The review of Morice's book suggests a good sound novel in a similar vein, though stylistically less scintillating. The review of the Keating book says nothing specific about the quality of the novel, letting the three-star rating and the reader's presumed previous knowledge of the popular Inspector Ghote (whose cases occasionally appear in *EQMM*) carry the load. The tone of the review, however, suggests the book's light touch and the gently farcical quality of Ghote's cases.

Though "The Jury Box" seldom carries an outright pan of any book, it often notes books with good features that have fallen down in some department. Two examples from the same column follow:

Playwright Bob Randall's *The Fan* (Random House, $7.95) tells the story of a Broadway musical star terrorized by a psychopathic fan. The narrative format (all letters between the characters) is sometimes awkward and ultimately unsatisfactory, but the book is readable and often suspenseful. (**)

A party seeking monsters in a Scottish loch figures in Gladys Mitchell's *Winking at the Brim* (McKay-Washburn, $6.95), second novel in the U.S. revival of Dame Beatrice Bradley's cases. Though there is fun along the way, a rather limp and perfunctory summing up makes it less impressive than *Watson's Choice*. (**)

While indicating quite specifically what the reviewer thinks went wrong, the two reviews note what is interesting about the books and try to strike a somewhat positive note. The Mitchell review suggests a below-par performance by a good writer and alludes to an earlier, better title. When possible, this practice can take the sting out of a bad review.

BRIGITTE WEEKS is the managing editor of *The Washington Post* "Book World."

15 | The Weekly Book Review Section

by BRIGITTE WEEKS

EVERY YEAR I read hundreds of competent book reviews, and I read hundreds of flawed, boring or ill-considered reviews. I also read a very small number—maybe a couple of dozen a year—that are outstanding, the perfect match of reviewer and book, one writer speaking to another, or one writer taking issue with another, clarifying and illuminating the issues as he does so. However, a brilliant writer can make a disastrous book reviewer. The ability to analyze and evaluate someone else's writing and to capture the flavor of the book does not rise from the same creative spring as the ability to write the books themselves. All the same, the most authoritative and informed book review will remain unread unless interesting and well expressed.

How does an outstanding review come to be? Some techniques of good book reviewing are straightforward. Read the book carefully, twice if necessary. (Mark everything especially interesting as you go along, because one forgets, and later, when the paper is finally in your typewriter, it is often impossible to find just the quotation or fact needed to illustrate a point.) Then let the book settle. This is a hard process to describe. It can take a few hours or weeks. Sometimes no time is enough, and often deadlines or publication dates will not wait. But while one is about one's daily business some thoughts about the book rise to the surface of the mind. Others sink away as unimportant or merely quibbles (a word reviewers *love*). It may be satisfying to a reviewer to spot that the main character used the wrong shackle to rig his sailboat when he was supposed to be an old salt; but if the rest of the story is an outstanding sea adventure, it may not be worth the space to explain the technical error (unless, of course, the review is for a sailing journal).

If the reviewer's reaction to the book is favorable, the piece is easier and more fun to write; but if it is negative, it is important to unravel reactions, pin down sources of these aggravations. Where did the story lose the reader? Where did the thesis of the book break down? How did the author alienate his audience? Negative reviews are not easy to write. It is hard to be both interesting and critical. There is no point in turning a machine gun on a mosquito. Unless it is in the public interest to expose errors or to qualify the reputation of an established writer, it is better to ignore bad books. There is never enough space to notice the good ones. Most editors will respect and appreciate the reviewer who reads a book and lets them know that space would be wasted on it.

Many of the "secrets" of good book reviewing involve resisting almost irresistible temptations: resist the temptation to use the book review as a soapbox to propagate pet theories—unless they are directly relevant. Readers want to know about the book under consideration, and with a very few exceptions they are not interested in the reviewer except as a thermometer to test the water before they jump in and read the book.

Resist what I have come to think of as "the detachable lead." This is one of the most common problems with a book review. For example, when reviewing an analysis of the 1976 Democratic Convention, don't use the first page of the review to survey the history of presidential elections or muse on the glut of political books this year. Don't talk for two pages about the progress of 20th-century poetry when considering a new volume by John Ashbery. When the piece is finished, look again at the first paragraph. Is the name of the book you are reviewing mentioned? Will the reader think you are feeling your way toward the book through a thicket of words? Could the review start just as well with paragraph two, as is often the case?

The reviewer's judgment of the book is crucial. Without it the review is nothing more than a précis of the plot or the argument. The reviewer also has an obligation to capture the flavor of the book, whether or not he likes it. He or she should enable the reader to make an informed guess—without prolonged plot summary—at how much he would enjoy the book. Even while disagreeing with Ralph Nader's theories on the safety of atomic energy, for example, the reviewer should make clear what areas Nader addresses and the scope of the book. Some attempt should be made to place an established writer in the context of his other work. This need not involve a merit rating but should give a general feeling of whether, for instance, Margaret Drabble's new novel is as good as her last, better, or whether it breaks new ground. It is important to be familiar with the body of work of the author being reviewed, although, under stress of deadline, it is often impossible to read everything by a prolific writer. Anyway, read something else by him or her.

Is any special preparation needed before launching into the first review? Endless, insatiable reading is probably the only basic training; the rest comes from writing and rewriting reviews and in reading published reviews, especially of books that you have read yourself. Develop special interests, become well versed in a particular kind of fiction, or in books on families, or self-help, or India, or whatever, to increase the base of judgment and add authority to your work. Only a rare reviewer can turn his or her hand to any topic, fiction or nonfiction, with equal success. It is important to identify your strong areas of interest and to exploit them. Most reviewers have professional expertise, and personal interests are equally valuable. I have an adopted son and am naturally interested in books on adoption, have a fair general knowledge of the field, and want to review a book with a new perspective or fresh information. An avid reader of Iris Murdoch, I have reviewed several of her novels. A new book of hers is read in light of several years of accumulated knowledge. But this too has its pitfalls—of programmed responses and lack of fresh insights. Editors and reviewers have to watch for repetition or staleness both in the author and in themselves.

How do book reviewers get selected? Where do they begin? Questions I am often asked, even though I can give no one answer, no straightforward method of qualifying, no clear-cut selection process. The usual method of getting started is to write to a book review editor, enclosing clips of your published reviews, and suggest a forthcoming title you would like to review, saying briefly why. This sometimes works, especially if the suggestion is well timed and accompanied by a set of competently written clips of your reviews. And if you don't have any clips, start reviewing for any publication that will print you, regardless of pay—

college papers, local newspapers, quarterlies, little magazines . . .

A riskier and more time-consuming method than the query letter and one that editors advocate at their peril is one more likely to get a review into print. Pick a forthcoming title, write a review, and send it to the editor, making sure it is the length and style that publication regularly uses. The book may have already been assigned to a reviewer. The book section may not want to review it at all. The editor may not like your review. But there is a chance, a slim but real chance, that if the review fills an existing need it may be used, and the first difficult step will have been taken. (Information on books to be published can be obtained from the trade journal, *Publishers Weekly*, or from publishers' catalogues. Ask the publisher for an advance copy or a set of galleys. They may not send them to you, but keep trying, or borrow the book from another reviewer or a book section editor willing to give a new reviewer a chance.)

Once you have some of your reviews in print, don't wait to be asked to review; make other suggestions—modest ones. With only one fiction review to your credit, it's not much good asking a leading book section editor if you can review the new novel by John Updike. And don't pester editors, or they will be unlikely to respond favorably. Dealing with requests to review takes up an enormous amount of a book editor's time. Brief, appropriate requests are appreciated, as are clean copy, correct spelling, immaculate accuracy in facts and names, a short identification, if necessary, and copy the right length. Writing 1,200 words when 600 are required is a sure way not to be asked to review again. All this will not get a bad review into print, but it will certainly give your work the best chance in an overcrowded marketplace. Good reviewers are in short supply despite the large numbers of hopefuls, and interesting, well-written, competent, and punctual reviews are rare. Genius is almost never ignored and is more likely to be courted by several editors than left to starve in a garret.

Who are these editors, and how do they decide what books to review and who should review them? Do famous authors always get reviewed? Do struggling experimental writers always get ignored by the crass commercial establishment? Questions often asked and which I can only answer here from my own experience. Book review editors come from incredibly diverse backgrounds. About the only thing they have in common is a love of books, a fascination with the written word. I worked for large publishing houses, as a book rewrite person, as a free-lance journalist, and as a magazine editor, before I became a book review editor. Most editors write reviews themselves from time to time. It serves as a salutary reminder of how hard it is to be brief, informative and to put your judgment on the line.

Assigning books to reviewers is a key job in a book review section. Everything depends on that process. A complex series of choices are involved: which books to review (*The Washington Post* "Book World" mentions about 2,000 a year and about 40,000 are published) and who should review those few selected. Some specialized reviewers may be called on only once every few years when a book on, say, cybernetics or stone circles is written for the general reader. Some reviewers work regularly on a large range of general-interest books; some review only fiction or only poetry. Experience and a close knowledge of the books and the reviewers is the only preparation for making good assignments, and it is easy to be wrong. Someone whose talents may seem perfectly matched to the book may be a rambling, dis-

organized reviewer or may be reluctant to come to any firm
judgment.

An editor must avoid programming a review by assigning
a book to someone whose hostility to the author's viewpoint
is already a matter of public record, or the author may claim
that his book was never given a fair chance. Editors must
scrupulously avoid—and this is hard—even the faintest
appearance of conflict of interest. The reviewer may be just
about to publish his own book on the subject and want to
demolish a prospective rival. He may be mentioned in the
book in glowing terms, and this would cast doubt on the
objectivity of a favorable review. The author of the book
may acknowledge the reviewer's help or may be a friend or
colleague of his. A good reviewer is alert to the problem and
will bring to the editor's attention any possible conflict
before accepting an assignment, but the final responsibility
for the integrity of the review must lie with the editor who
prints it.

An equally fundamental choice is how to select books for
full review, for mention in a column, for a short notice, or
for no attention at all. Once more, this is no clear-cut
process: some books must be reviewed. They are written by
authors of established fame, a Cheever or a Galbraith, or
deal with events of interest to many readers, Watergate, or
the Middle East crisis. Some books are of local interest.
Books on government or foreign policy, for instance, have
a special claim to space in *The Washington Post.* Sometimes
a reviewer who is respected will suggest a book not previously considered for notice. Some books are brought to the
editor's attention by experts in their fields. No book editor
is omniscient. He must learn to choose his sources of advice
and information with care, to differentiate between publicity
people he can trust and those that routinely exaggerate the

glories of their list. All these are ingredients in the final decision. Some books are ignored that should be reviewed. Some books are reviewed that should have been ignored, but rarely, if ever, is a distinguished volume passed over by every book section, however unknown the author. Somewhere, somehow, on the literary underground the word gets out that here is something worth notice, and if an aspiring reviewer brings such a book to the attention of a book editor, his credibility moves up twenty points.

As I have tried to convey, the world of book reviewing is a complex one. The topography involves the original author of the book, his publisher and editor; then the book editor and his individual interests and judgments moves onto the map, followed by the reviewer, who brings his knowledge and skills to bear on the book he is assigned. The result of so many indefinables is obviously unpredictable, which may be the reason that only a dozen or so of the reviews that pass across my desk in the course of a year meet all the criteria of excellence. But for those who want to become book reviewers, the challenge of acting as the advance scout for the reading public is an endless and exciting one.

P. ALBERT DUHAMEL is Book Review Editor of
The Boston Herald American.

16

The Structure of a Book Review

by P. ALBERT DUHAMEL

A BOOK review is the expression of a writer's opinion about a book he or she has, presumably, recently read. Since no opinion is worth any more than the reason, or reasons, proffered in its support, the minimum essentials required for a good book review are: (1) a statement of a judgment about the book, and (2) some "because clause," or clauses, explaining how and why the writer reached that conclusion.

Book reviews without reasons supporting the evaluation of the book are but a series of exclamations over how much the writer liked, or disliked, the book. Such "reviews," delivered orally, reflecting the enthusiasms of a friend, may be tolerated, if we happen to share the same tastes. But book reviews written for a broad audience will be respected only if they reflect responsible, analytic, substantiated judgments. Anyone can speculate on the possibility of life on Mars or life after death, but the only speculators who won't be scoffed at are those who will support their guesses with evidence of some kind.

This does not imply that all book reviews must begin with a blunt, compressed summary of the argument, consisting of the main proposition and its "because clause," such as: "I didn't like this book because the plot didn't hold my attention." In some professional journals, like *Publishers Weekly* and *Library Journal*, which are read by librarians and book buyers searching for quick information and guidance about books worth buying, such flat reviews may be acceptable. But reviews intended for a general audience, such as those published in *Time* Magazine or *The New York Times*, must be written to interest any general reader, a reader who may not be particularly interested in the book being reviewed but who will pause to read the review as an independent, colorful essay that can stand on its own.

To catch the attention of the general reader, a book review has to open with a "grabber," an opening, lead sentence which grabs readers by the lapels and says, in effect, "Listen!" If the book being reviewed is a novel, one way of achieving this effect is to open with a summary of the plot up to some critical point. I once began a review of an historical novel, *The Iron King*, with this gambit: "As flames wreathed his face and set his hair alight, the Grand Master of the Knights Templar summoned the Pope, Clement, the King of France, Philip, and his Secretary, to face divine judgment for their acts. Within the year, all three were dead." It would be difficult not to read on for a paragraph or two to learn more about this book.

Another means of opening a review to "hook" the reader is by teasing him with some intriguing words or details. A review of *Mahatma Gandhi and His Apostles* began: "Dhoti clad, walking with his arms around the shoulders of the two teen-aged, sari-clad nieces whom he called his 'walking sticks,' Bapuji gave little indication to his closest disciples of the extremes to which his practice of brahmachari had carried him."

After an intriguing opening—startling detail, paradoxical statement, outrageous exaggeration—a review can usually continue to hold a reader's interest with some kind of summary of the plot or contents of the book. In the course of the summary, the critic can gradually reveal his opinion of the book, letting it out a little at a time as a novelist reveals his plot. Gradually, he can also indicate the reasons behind the opinion, usually suggested by sentences that begin, "Had he included a fuller treatment . . ." So the reviewer is saying, in effect, "I don't think this book is as good as it might have been if the treatment had been more complete."

Another kind of sentence frequently used by a reviewer to indicate the book's weaknesses, with a supporting reason, may take this form: Compared to Bruce Catton's *A Stillness at Appomattox*, this history of the Civil War seems slow-paced, deficient in detail. . . ." Comparing or contrasting a book with a generally accepted classic on the same subject constitutes a very effective means of demonstrating why an opinion for or against a book is not just personal, subjective, or a matter of taste.

There is no way to catalogue the reasons that may be cited in support of a favorable or an adverse judgment of a book, or of any work of art, for that matter. Among the most common reasons given for liking or disliking a novel, however, are the strengths or weaknesses of the plot. A reviewer who points out that he did not like a novel because the story was not properly paced, because there was no explanation of the conflict among the characters, because there was no suspense, is invoking traditional criteria of judgment.

Similarly, if the novel does not seem to have been intended to tell a story, but rather to portray a character and if the reviewer has some reservations about the credibility of the people depicted in it, other readers will respond in the same way. There is a danger to be avoided here, however: The test of acceptability of a character cannot be only the individual reviewer's experience. Few of us have known heroes as aged as King Lear, as paranoid as Ahab, as "physical" as Hemingway's characters, but we can conceive of them as falling within human experience, and that's what we must invoke in judgment, not our own personal, parochial experience.

In evaluating a nonfiction book, the reasons for approving or disapproving are most often concerned with the completeness of the coverage of its subject or the clarity of its style. A book on economics, for example, might be an encyclopedia of wisdom on its subject, but a reader might be justified in considering it deficient because its style is murky, its organization difficult to follow, its presentation on a level so difficult as to be understood only by experts. A book on history could be applauded or criticized because it did or did not cover its subject thoroughly. The potential reviewer might have read it asking himself questions like these: Are all the events leading up to the battle clear? Are the consequences or the aftermath described in detail? If not, the reviewer then has objective reasons for considering the book wanting. Above all, the reviewer must try to avoid citing only personal reasons, matters of taste or pique, in support of his judgment.

Reviews of books on politics or of biographies need careful handling so the critic doesn't end up writing, in effect, that he disliked the book because the writer's politics are not *his* politics or the beliefs of the subject were not his beliefs. A reviewer who criticizes a book because it disagrees with his assumptions or commitments is begging his readers to agree with his prejudices.

One way out of this dangerous gambit is to try to determine the purpose of the book, say a biography on Lawrence of Arabia. If it can be determined that the biographer's intention was to explain the effect of Lawrence's early life upon his later sexual aberrations, then the book ought to be judged on the extent to which the biographer realized his intention, not on whether the writer's conclusions agree with the reviewer's. In other words, as a book reviewer, don't set out to evaluate the writer's assumptions or intentions. Grant him those, and judge the extent to which you think he realized them. Let your readers decide for themselves whether they think a book with such a purpose worth reading.

Related to this tactical posture of not asking your readers to substitute your value judgments for an author's value judgments is the obligation of making sure you review the book and not the author. Though you may know the author in some other connection as a good guy or a bad guy, such personal factors are irrelevant in judging a book. Also, don't become trivial, nit-picking over a misplaced apostrophe here, an incorrect use of *op. cit.* or *loc. cit.* You have more important matters to consider, and you don't have that much space to do it in.

Writing book reviews, though not like writing sonnets, is working in miniature. Few publications that publish book reviews use many running longer than 600 words. *The New York Times Book Review* and *The New York Review of Books* do publish in every issue some reviews of 1,500 words or more, but these are reviews of important books or books by important authors, and they are written by experienced and highly qualified reviewers. They not only review the specific book but describe the state of knowledge of the subject under discussion and may also assess the author's whole body of work up to the present.

Anyone starting out to learn how to write book reviews,

anyone hoping to have some book reviews published and to develop as an authority in a particular area, should think of writing 300- to 500-word reviews. In this constrained space, every word must be considered very carefully. Within this "narrow room," space must be found for an effective "lead," a summary of the contents of the book, plot or chapter topics, and some detailing of the reasons why the vote went for or against.

The best way to break into review writing is to develop some area of special competence. It need not be as recondite as Nepalese tantras, but it should also not be as hopelessly broad as "the novel." Instead, choose some special type of novel—the historical, the Gothic, the Victorian, the mystery—that may be based on your previous experience, and read around in it until you feel you know the territory and can write confidently: "Had so-and-so been as complete as ——— ——————," or "Compared to so-and-so, this story limps. . . ." Then you can write to an editor of a publication using book reviews, stating your special interests and knowledge and asking if you may try a review of a book in that particular area. A week—or a year—may pass before you are given a chance, depending upon whether the editor has some established reviewer in your field, or if there is a spate of books of that type being published. But chances are that if you write to several editors, you will be given an opportunity at some point to review a book.

Whether you get a chance to review a book right away or not, I think you should train yourself to write book reviews by keeping notebooks. All too often we read a book and so completely forget it that when we try to recommend it to a friend we don't know why, or what made it seem outstanding. Writing a review, for a scrapbook or for a file, will make you a better reader, a better writer, a better critic.

BARBARA ELLEMAN is Children's Book Reviewer
for *The Booklist* (a publication of the American
Library Association), an active member of the
Society of Children's Book Writers, a free-lance
reviewer, and a frequent speaker on book reviewing and children's books.

17 Reviewing Children's Books
by BARBARA ELLEMAN

THE REVIEWING of children's books differs from reviewing
books for adults because of the nature of the market. This
is not to imply that different criteria are used in evaluating
children's books; on the contrary, the upgrading of books
for young readers is something that for years many knowledgeable people in the field have been striving for. The differences result from two inherent facts. First, children's
books are written, edited, published, reviewed, and purchased
by adults, for children—a situation that does not exist in the
adult market, and one that frequently sets off the widely
debated question of the importance of child appeal in a book.
Pragmatists look only for books that children will read,
whereas purists search only for books of high literary quality, but without regard to children's interests. Fortunately,
most children's books waver somewhere in the middle.

Second, the adult market is determined mainly through
bookstores, but this is not true with children's books. In
fact, 85% to 90% of all children's books are purchased

each year by librarians and are selected mainly from reviews in only four major publications (*Booklist, Bulletin of the Center for Children's Books, The Horn Book,* and *School Library Journal*). Few popular magazines or newspapers review children's books, and if they do, it is only on a limited scale. Advertisements of children's books, again in contrast to adult books, are rarely seen by the lay public. Bookstores comprise a very small part of the children's book market, and child book buyers are virtually non-existent. Although large school and public libraries are able to examine books prior to purchase, and some journals do carry reviews, the majority of librarians must rely on the above-mentioned professional magazines for comprehensive coverage. To receive a poor review or none at all (*The Horn Book,* for example, is selective; *Booklist* reviews only those materials it recommends) is to lessen greatly a book's chance to succeed commercially and to find its way into the hands of children.

It is a heavy responsibility to know that the cumulative effort of hours of creative work on the part of the author and the financial commitment from the publisher are held in the balance, if only partially, in a reviewer's hands. On the other side, librarians with tight budgets are calling for critical analysis, continually challenging reviewers to help them use their limited money judiciously.

This brings me to the make-up of the review itself, the writing of those few words which translate the creative work of the author into a selection tool for the librarian buying the books that children will eventually read.

An effective book review is well written, is informative, and conveys to the reader a sense of the author's purpose. Not only should a review capsulate the plot, summarize the contents (in the case of nonfiction), describe the graphic elements, and comment on the literary qualities and format, but it should also suggest an underlying tone that reflects the book's style and leaves the reader with an impression of the book's intrinsic value.

If this is what comprises a book review, how does a reviewer go about shaping his thoughts in order to get the total impression concisely on the page? For me, it comes in three stages: reading the book; mulling over in my mind, for example, the tangled pieces of plot, images of character, atmosphere of the setting, and tone of the work; and finally, writing the review. Often it is necessary to remove myself from the book, to stand back and look at it impersonally; sometimes even to let a day lapse before the writing begins. This is to insure that I am not swept along in a tide of personal preferences, built-in prejudices, or memories of past works by familiar authors or illustrators.

Reviewing requires an impartial approach—a careful exploration of how, where, and why an author employed a certain element, motif or action; an examination of the writer's craft, consciously looking for nuances of technique that make a work distinctive; and the ability to read beyond the plot devices and character portrayals to what the author is attempting to say.

I try to look at each book I review in four separate ways before combining my thoughts into a concrete written statement. The mulling-over process includes pinpointing the author's theme, scrutinizing the overall impact, projecting the book's child appeal, and delineating the literary qualities.

Whether fiction, nonfiction, picture book, or novel, the book's *raison d'être* must be apparent and true to its original premise; the development must be consistent and logical; and the theme, especially in fiction, should unfold carefully and with credibility. However, the theme must not stick out, crying "message," which will only turn children off;

neither should the theme be so buried under endless narrative, floundering plot development, or extraneous characters that children will miss the author's main point. In a high fantasy, if good and evil are being personified as black or white characters, then the author must not confuse his audience with sudden shadings of gray. Conversely, a realistic novel attempting to portray a ghetto must have rounded characters with blendings of both good and bad qualities. A light adventure story may be written to entertain; if so, a moral dropped into the final pages seems jarring.

Themes begun in opening chapters and carelessly changed midstream, dropped entirely from a book or dissipated in the final pages, are irritating to readers and leave them feeling that they are being cheated out of a full-fledged story. The theme that is memorable enlarges our understanding and is one that readers discover for themselves, not one delivered didactically by the author. English author Penelope Lively has said that she strives for plots that are like the tips of icebergs with themes that lie below the surface, lingering in a child's mind long after the story is finished.

When authors aren't writing out of their own deep feelings, contrivance often results. This is clearly recognizable when a story doesn't develop naturally out of the characters' own personalities, time, and setting, but relies on situations set up by the author or occurring out of context. In life, strange coincidences do occur, but in a plot line, incidents must be believable within the story's limits. An author who builds to a climax with the characters leading the way, letting the story be told through their actions and dialogue, will create a stronger plot. Underplaying, simplicity, and subtlety are key words to remember.

Nonfiction is not exempt; if an author wants to give

children a scientific examination of the milkweed plant but provides no table of contents, index, or labeled photographs, the writer's purpose, despite competent writing, is suspect, as he has not provided researchers with an easy way to extract the material. Or, a book on caves that rambles in a superficial way, neglecting specifics, such as origins, development, location, and wildlife within, should be noted as unsatisfactory.

Not only is it important to question what the author is trying to say, but also to ask whether the author succeeded in saying it. Although the purpose might be clear (as in the book about milkweeds), the answer to the second question must be no, because the author failed to fulfill his purpose. Other examples might be a picture book that has artistic illustrations but a weak, fragmented story; a satisfactorily designed craft book that gives incomplete directions; a realistic novel that closes with a syrupy ending; or a biography that only glamorizes the subject's life. Details of format—type, paper, layout, and design; the presence of bibliographies, indexes, and glossaries; clarity of photographs, maps and diagrams; and use of illustrations—all need to be scrutinized for their part in the total impact of the book.

Judging whether a book will appeal to children is difficult. My fifteen years' experience as a school and public librarian provides me with a broad basis for understanding children's needs, likes, and dislikes. Although I know I can misjudge and am aware of the wide differences in children's backgrounds, tastes, and preferences, I feel certain that children are more alike than different. When a story has a feeling of excitement, a naturalness about it, a quick plunge into the plot, sparkling dialogue, and a swift pace, it's on its way to finding a wide audience of children.

In nonfiction books, accessible material, inviting formats, and helpful illustrations or photographs are basic to the kind of smooth-flowing writing that pulls a reader in from the outset. Information must be presented in a lively manner, free of condescension.

Although reviewers sometimes differ in their interpretations of what a book is about, how successful the author has been, and what the child-appeal factor is, there are specific points to discuss when considering literary quality. Criticism is based on elements such as the development of character, flow of plot line, function of setting, consistency of point of view, devices of transition, and sense of tone.

Intrusion of sentimentality in the plot, I find, is a bothersome factor in children's books. Some adult writers, either thinking to protect children from a harsh world or remembering a childhood that might have been, present Pollyanna characters in candy-coated worlds that fail to ring true. Fear of letting children face anything but humdrum situations can result in bland plots lacking action and tension.

On the other hand, authors who strive to compete with television by creating sensationalized plots that rely on outrageous, frantic situations, detailed violence, or specific sexual encounters are equally amiss in offering children less than the best.

Stereotyping is a major factor to be considered when examining a book. Realistic characters should be drawn like real people so that children learn to recognize through their reading that no one is all good or all bad. Reviewers need to analyze carefully generalizations of ethnic characters, as well as careless portrayals of specific groups, such as the aged, the handicapped, politicians, or teachers.

It is in examining these various elements that a reviewer must come to grips with the book's essence and must balance its flaws against its strengths, being careful to give the book a thoughtful and fair judgment. In an article entitled, "The Critic and Children's Literature" Elizabeth Nesbitt once said, "For it is true that a book may have weaknesses, but at the same time accomplish something so positive, so worthwhile, so constructive as to negate its faults." This is an important point to remember, because sometimes one element can be bothersome to the point of being a prevailing influence in the total appraisal of the work. It can be difficult to keep personal opinion about an author's previous work, one's individual taste for a particular genre, or a fondness, for example, for the book's setting, from swaying judgment. But this is a part of reviewing and must be grappled with.

Once the mulling-over process is complete and the decisions are made as to the author's purpose, the overall impressions, the child-appeal factor, and the specifics of the literary quality, it is time to begin writing the review.

It is imperative to keep in mind that readers will not have the book in front of them, and any remarks made about the dust jacket, format, general appearance, and illustrative material must be extremely clear. This is particularly true in regard to picture books, where half of the total effect depends on the illustrations. Both descriptive and critical comment should be included. Note should be made, for example, if the artistic qualities do not match the tone of the story.

The content or plot should be briefly but substantially outlined, without cluttering up the reader's mind with extraneous information. The critical comment needs to incorporate in a concise, orderly way all that has been mentioned, with the reviewer staying decidedly in the background, and, if possible, letting a touch of the author's tone and style show through.

With some 2,500 children's books published each year, it

would be easy to dismiss some with a "this is another book on. . . ." But that isn't fair. Each book needs to be examined, evaluated, and described for its own intrinsic worth. If at all possible, I try to find the "positive" element, as Elizabeth Nesbitt so adroitly put it. While judging critically in a constructive way, I act as a bridge from the creative work of author and publisher to the librarians and children who are buying and reading the books.

TERRY ANDERSON is Book Editor of *The Denver Post*.

18

The Regional Book Section

by TERRY ANDERSON

THE BOOK review section of *The Denver Post* is the only one of its kind in the Rocky Mountain region and perhaps the largest section between Chicago and Los Angeles.

The Sunday book section, from three to five pages long, appears in the tabloid *Roundup Magazine*. In addition, non-fiction reviews appear three times weekly on the Op-Ed page. There are also three special sections each year—a children's issue in the spring and fall and a November Christmas issue which reviews gift books.

Because of limited space, *The Post* reviews only a small percentage of the more than 4,000 books it receives a year. Consequently, the book section attempts to give its readers a representative cross-section. The section not only reviews books of national importance, but also books about the West and books written by regional authors.

For example, the paper this year has reviewed books by such noted authors as Robert Penn Warren, Shirley Ann Grau, Joan Didion, John Cheever, and John Kenneth Galbraith. These writers receive attention because the mere fact that they have written books—no matter how good or bad—is news, and news is sometimes just as important to the book section as the reviews themselves.

At the same time, *The Post* has prominently featured books and authors that may receive little national attention, because their appeal is mainly regional. Such regional books, however, are reviewed in *The Post* because they are important to the West. This list has included biographies about such diverse individuals as Charles Boettcher, Jack Dempsey, and Gene Fowler; books about railroads, conservation and Indians; and books by local authors about mystery, finance and architecture. There have also been profiles about authors like Judith Viorst, Richard Bach, Clive Cussler, Kay Wilson Klem, and Dan Jorgensen, the latter three all Colorado authors.

The Post reviews over 800 books a year, all reviewers being local, part-time, free-lance writers. Most of the reviewing staff of forty or more writers have had a long association with the newspaper, although most of the reviews are written by fewer than a dozen people. The rest are only occasional contributors. For the most part they are specialists. One reviews biographies; another nothing but religion; another only feminist literature; and still another, just books on the West.

Finding competent reviewers for fiction is one of the hardest task facing most book editors. Fiction is so intangible that some reviewers find it difficult to decide how much of the plot to summarize in a review; where to begin commenting on the author's style; and when to make comparisons either with a writer's previous work or with that of other writers. The biggest fault in reviewers of fiction is a failure to be specific about what the author accomplishes in the novel.

Consider, for example, the following two reviews:

As *A Certain Man,* Arley becomes a father. But he is never sure he is good enough for this job either. His son breaks away from the church and his daughter tires of his endless concern for others and is soon off doing her own thing. Annah also tires of ladies' aid work and gets a job to be her own person—against Arley's wishes. When Arley dies unexpectedly and alone, we ponder his fate, but he will be remembered by the thousands of parishioners he embraced and the readers of this tale.

(Bruce) Ducker is a lawyer, and there are times when he writes like one. He is more interested in giving information and leading the reader through the financial machinations of his plot than he is in building mood and character. His characters for the most part are flat, and the reader has little idea even what they look like. But these flaws really don't detract from the book because the 1960s were an impersonal time for business—when business leaders were one-dimensional, when ideas and actions were more important than what they did to individuals. . . . (It) is an absorbing book for anyone who, like Tom Swalleck, is both fascinated and frightened of the power of the young men of go-go years. It is even more appealing to Denverites, who, knowing this is fiction, nevertheless, will attempt to glimpse the personalities of 17th Street in Ducker's work.

Both examples are conclusions of book reviews that have appeared in *The Post*. The first example is vague and too plot-oriented, while the second is quite specific and concrete.

The first example is not a good conclusion for a book review for many reasons. The reviewer says little about the character of Arley and nothing about the author's style of writing, and there are no specifics about what is good or bad about the novel. Consequently, the reviewer leaves the reader feeling vague about wanting to read the book.

The second review wraps everything up into a neat package for the reader. The writer tells something about the author, his style of writing, character development, the book's relevancy to the real world, and why the book might appeal to potential readers. The conclusion gives the reader enough information to help him decide whether or not he wants to either read or buy the book. This is what a good review should do.

Needless to say, the writer of the first review does little review work for *The Post*. The second reviewer is called upon quite often to write major reviews for the paper.

A good reviewer should convey to his audience at least two basic things—what the book is about and whether or not it is worth reading—and tell it in an entertaining way, no matter what the verdict on the book. The review must have a point of its own, with lively, concrete details to support any conclusion by the reviewer.

The best reviews—as in the second example above—must furnish some perspective on the book and either advance a reader's appreciation of the book or challenge it in some way. The well-informed reviewer must not be afraid to praise, attack, or even demolish a book. He must never hedge in expressing his opinion candidly, because that is unfair to the reader and the author; failure to be frank detracts from a writer's credibility as a reviewer.

To judge the merits of a book, the reviewer must ask himself many questions as he reads the book. What is the author bringing to the book as a writer and thinker? What is he trying to do, and has he realized that goal? Where has he succeeded or failed? Has he made any contribution to the advancement of knowledge? Where does this book fit into his previous works? Is the writer as concerned about the individual word as he is about the content of the book?

As important as the body and the conclusions of a review are, a good introduction is essential in order to attract the reader's attention in the first place. The reviewer must tantalize the reader with a question, a startling fact, some important episode, or perhaps with a quotation from the book:

Consider these openers:

1) If an American college offered a graduate course on Turkish justice *Midnight Express* would be its bible.

2) Trying to decide if *My Story* is for real can take just about as much time as reading the book. And then you still aren't likely to come away with any conclusive answer except that, if Judith Exner's description of events is true, it is an incredible indictment.

3) They rose from playing club dates at $20 a night to become Hollywood's most famous straight-man-and-stooge act. At the pinnacle, they earned $2 million a year through movies, radio and appearances. They died broke.

4) Every generation, writes Philip Caputo, is doomed to fight its war, to endure the same old experiences, suffer the loss of the same old illusions, and learn the same old lessons.

Readers will want to know why the first book is a bible on the Turkish justice system. In the second example, the reviewer offers the reader a choice about Exner's credibility. In the third, the reader wonders how Bud Abbott and Lou Costello lost all that money. In the last example, the reader wants to find out which war and which generation Caputo wants to write about. Each opener is different, yet each accomplishes the task of enticing the reader into the review. In each case the reviewer justifies his opening remarks in the body of the review without giving the book away.

The Post feels its editorial content must speak for and be representative of the readers in the Rocky Mountain region. The same is true of the book section. *The Post* feels its book readers want to know how local book reviewers feel about books of national importance and what other readers in the area are reading. But they also want to know what is happening elsewhere in the world of books. The book section attempts to satisfy those demands in a variety of ways.

The newspaper does not use any national wire copy or celebrity reviews, nor does it run any national best seller list. Instead, all book reviews are written locally; the best seller lists are compiled by two local wholesale book jobbers; and a book column keeps readers abreast of the world of books both locally and nationally. Consequently, there is a steady market for local part-time, free-lance reviewers, not only because of the paper's editorial policy but also because reviewers come and go.

The best way for a reviewer to become part of *The Post*'s book review staff is to submit a letter with a sample of other published writing, reviews or a sample review of some current book. Areas of special interest or expertise should also be mentioned. Finally, the closer the writer lives to Denver, the better his or her chances of being added to the staff. Writing reviews for *The Post* is less than lucrative, however, because the budget is small. Reviewers can expect to keep the review copy of the book and often pick up books that aren't going to be reviewed. Also, reviewers will have the satisfaction of knowing that they are shaping the tastes of their readers. By continually offering their opinions on books, they become a strong influence in developing readers' tastes.

In addition to book reviews, LUCAS LONGO has written short stories, poetry, children's books, plays, and a novel, *The Family on Vendetta Street* (Doubleday).

19 | Book Reviewing: Pathway to Publication

by LUCAS LONGO

FOR THE unpublished, free-lance writer, there are many ways into print. I learned very early in my writing career that one of the best ways to get writing credits is to review books. The rewards are modest, and the work is hard, but the beginning writer stands a good chance of getting a start as a free lancer with book reviewing.

The unpublished writer might break into print in a publication by sending a letter to the "letters to the editor" column. Almost every newspaper and magazine has a section devoted to letters from readers, and if your letter is published, you're on your way to making editors know that you exist. You might then send a query letter informing the editor of your interest in reviewing books, giving fully your schooling and background.

A good place to start is with periodicals in which you can use your ethnic background. I started by trying the Italian-American newspapers and magazines. Editors assume, and justly, that if you were born and bred in a certain ethnic environment, you will understand that background better than someone who was not. I had my first review in *The Italian-American Times,* a Bronx weekly. Using this review as a sample of my work, I wrote to other publications. *La Parola del Popola,* a Chicago-based labor magazine, then sent me a book to review. When I queried that magazine, besides emphasizing my Italian background, I mentioned that I had been a longshoreman and a union member, which made my query for this labor publication even stronger. With Xeroxed copies of these two reviews to show, I continued my search for more markets. I found another outlet in *Gaceta,* a newspaper in Tampa, Florida, and then went on to more and more publications.

After the ethnic-oriented periodicals, the next step is to query small general newspapers and magazines which do not pay but will help you build up an impressive list of reviews. And often, when you do good work, you may receive a small check. There are many small specialized publications, too, that use reviews of books in their fields of interest. For example, *Review of Books and Religion,* in Belmont, Vermont, is receptive to the amateur.

If you are well informed in a special field, be sure to let the editor know. It may be a hobby, farming, auto mechanics, or, as in my case, poetry and social work. Almost any area in which you have special information will soon bring you a book to review. If you know about motorcycles, for example, an editor is likely to have you review a book about bikes. If you know a certain region of the country well, an editor may be willing to send you a novel depicting that area. Always indicate in query letters whatever special skills or experience you have. When we moved to New Haven, Connecticut, I visited the editor of the "Art & Leisure" section of *The New Haven Register.* That led to my becoming that paper's regular reviewer for all books about Italian-American subjects and authors.

As I have suggested, the market for the newcomer in book reviewing is large. Many editors, including those of big-name magazines, do not like to use the same reviewer too often, and this means that the welcome mat is out for the unknown and unpublished reviewer. Even the established reviewer has to be constantly seeking new outlets. *The Nation, The Centennial Review, The Ohio Review* are magazines with liberal policies toward the new writer. Scholarly magazines also are receptive to unpublished writers, if the subject of the book to be reviewed is known to the reviewer. For instance, my graduate thesis on Thomas Wolfe as a playwright opened the doors for me to review for *The Southern Review.*

Certain tools are necessary for the book reviewer. You will need to keep on your shelf information about current markets. Read other book reviews. Step by step, you can make book reviewing a full-time occupation or let it serve you as a steady sideline. After a time and considerable experience in reviewing, I was able to convince the publisher of a weekly newspaper in Brooklyn that a book review column would add prestige to his newspaper and bring in more advertising revenue from bookstores and publishers. I had been to see several bookstore owners who liked the idea, and I shared this information with the newspaper's editor. Thus I began my weekly column, "Literary Lights," for *The Bensonhurst News.* At first I received no money. Today I am paid fifty dollars for every column.

Chances are that if you want to be a writer, you won't want to be a book reviewer the rest of your days. But as a beginning, book reviewing can bring satisfaction. Seeing your by-line over published book reviews will help you overcome despair from rejections. Also, reading will keep you in touch with what publishers are looking for, and your horizons will be broadened. For example, I was never partial to the suspense novel or the Gothic, but I have learned to respect both. My personal tastes run to serious fiction and poetry, yet to be an honest reviewer, one has to learn to respect the craft of every form of literature. In reviewing Bill Pronzini's book *Snowbound*, I became aware that in almost ten years as a book reviewer, I had achieved the necessary sense of objectivity. While this novel was not my cup of tea, I saw that it would be dishonest to deny the pleasure it could bring to the huge number of readers who love suspense yarns, and I gave the book the rave it deserved. Even in the case of nonfiction, when the subject matter is not to my liking, I find that I am able to render a fair verdict. Sometimes a subject I do not like is presented in a book so effectively that my curiosity is aroused.

I do not want to sound pompous by offering a lot of precepts. But I do want to share with the amateur an experience which has worked for me and all those who are now selling. It goes without saying that the craft of writing is only for those who can genuinely sustain excitement. But even if you have never sold a single line, you may get your start in book reviewing.

1. Do follow the word requirements; a little shorter is better. Count, do not estimate, the words.
2. Mention title of book, author, publisher, price. If nonfiction, name all who were involved in the writing, including translators; in documentaries, list all editors concerned.
3. Indicate the kind of book it is—Gothic, black comedy, serious novel, etc. If essays, indicate subjects covered.

4. Give the time of the story.

5. Indicate place of action and the setting.

6. Supply information about characters, and say something about the author. If history, tell how other authors treated the same subject. Do the same for biography.

7. Discuss style and contents, always objectively.

8. Do not reveal key matters of narrative or plot. On the other hand, convey your enthusiasm or distaste, or both—honestly and objectively, of course.

9. Make sure your review is a review of the book, and not a review of your own ideas, aesthetic or otherwise. Many book editors consider the latter as the cardinal sin.

10. Use your very best prose. Make every effort to achieve balance, not too elaborate in some sections, too sketchy elsewhere.

11. Be sure the review arrives in good condition, signed and on time, and directed to the proper person at the publication.

12. Return pictures sent by the editor with the book.

13. If you cannot handle an assignment, return the book to the editor at once.

14. When reviewing a book by an author with several other published books, mention them, if possible.

15. When reviewing a first book, mention something about the author's background and other writing achievements.

16. All authors like to have reviewers perceive and note in the review what they were trying to do; it is on this basis that they prefer to be criticized.

Finally, I want to emphasize how important it is to place that first review. You will rank as a pro at once. I have indicated how, with earnest application, arduous to be sure but not impossible, you can achieve publication. But I also must stress the importance of producing quality work. The chances are that you have optimistic plans for your future in writing. By all means, add to this optimism, this ambition. Work with enthusiasm and confidence. Confidence comes from knowing your craft. This expertise will show in every line you write.

In book reviewing, whether you write full time or occasionally, study and persistence are required. You must be acquainted with the mechanics of your craft and have a broad view of the field. Don't restrict your reading only to books you intend to review. Writing for a living, or for fun, is not for the indolent. Before you try for publication, be sure you are qualified, or in reviewing a book, you could easily be reviewing your own ignorance.

This material is excerpted from a brochure prepared by the Children's Services Division of the Santiago (California) Library System and is reprinted here by permission.

20 | How to Review a Children's Book

To PARAPHRASE T. S. Eliot, "The rudiment of criticism is the ability to select a good book and reject a bad book; and its most severe test is its ability to select a good *new* book, to respond properly to a new situation."

The well-known specialist in children's literature, Zena Sutherland, points out these responsibilities of the children's book reviewer:

1. Be objective in your evalution of the book.
2. Be aware of controversial themes, sex mores, and unconventional language.
3. Know the field of children's literature so as to have a basis for evaluation.
4. Know children, their needs and wants.
5. Know the audience for whom the review is being written.
6. Judge each book on its own merit.
7. Read the book cover to cover!
8. Consider the book as a communication. Popularity and literary quality are *not* the same thing. Both

aspects must be taken into account; they should be in balance, and this balance should be carefully considered.

9. Compare this particular book with others in the genre or on the same subject or by the same author.
10. Be aware of the problem of translating a book into English:
    a. Is it true to the original text?
    b. Is it idiomatic?

When feasible, try to use the author's writing style, or a few of his or her words, phrases or sentences to help convey the flavor of the book. But do not paraphrase a plot or give detailed recapitulation of contents. Three or four sentences are enough; not more than one should be devoted to plot.

Watch for any biases:
1. Are sexual, racial, or age groups treated fairly?
2. How does the author's treatment of them affect the impact of the book?
3. Is the author's opinion presented as fact?

TYPES OF CHILDREN'S BOOKS

Picture books

The picture book at its best is a fusion of text and illustration. Illustrations should extend and interpret the story. Ask yourself the following questions about picture books you review:

1. Does the fusion work?
2. Will it work for children?
3. How do you evaluate the design, originality, art work, and appeal?
4. Do the mood and style of the pictures match the text?

Folklore

1. How good are they as stories?
2. How does this collection compare with others of the same kind?
3. Are the stories available in other collections?
4. Is it a book for children, or a book for folklorists?
5. Does the style reflect an oral tradition, or is this a literary treatment?
6. Do the stories and style truly represent the culture from which they come, or do they reflect a bias from the author's culture?
7. Are sources, parallels, or other relevant information provided?

Fables, myths, and epics

Older children are the primary audience for the pithy—if sometimes didactic—wisdom of the fables, although many individual fables have been skillfully presented in picture-story format. Children may not understand the complexity of symbolism in myths and legends, but they can appreciate the drama and beauty of the stories. The great epics can satisfy a child's need to admire deeds of high courage.

Poetry

Poetry should present a new perspective with an economy of well-chosen words.

1. Does the poetry speak *to* the child, not at or about him or her?
2. Evaluate poetry for its uniqueness and its use of language.
3. Check for variety in—
   a. meter—the number of feet in a line, or the com-

bination of the number and the kind of metrical feet (iambic pentameter, for instance).

b. rhyme—the repetition of sound at the ends of two or more lines or within lines.

c. scheme—pattern of rhyme within a poem.

d. type—

1) *lyric*—a short poem (ode, sonnet, etc.) usually with a musical quality

2) *narrative*—poems that tell a story and are usually rather long

3) *dramatic*—the pattern of rhyme within a poem

4. For an anthology of poetry, check the availability of the poems elsewhere.

Fiction

Here we can use the same criteria we bring to judging adult fiction—with some special additions relating to children's books:

1. Consider plot, characterization, and style.

2. Is the story absorbing, convincing, and carefully worked out to an honest conclusion?

3. Is it entertaining without being moralistic?

4. Will the reader meet real characters and watch them grow?

5. Good fiction should offer an appealing story, told smoothly, with freshness, and originality.

6. Compare the novel with previous work by the same author, or with books on the same theme by other authors.

7. From whose point of view is the story told?

8. Tell if the book is from one of these sub-categories:

a. humorous stories

b. mysteries

     c. animal stories
     d. historical fiction
     e. adventure tales
     f. realistic stories
  9. Complexity of plot development and concepts pre-
     sented should be geared to the level of the child's
     development.

Nonfiction

  1. Does the book aim toward high standards of literary
     quality?
  2. Is it accurate and current?
  3. Will it appeal to the audience for which it is geared?
  4. Do the illustrations clarify the text?
  5. Notice the presence or absence of
     a. tables
     b. maps
     c. appendices
     d. picture credits
     e. index
     f. glossary
     g. bibliographies
     h. table of contents
     i. suggestions for further reading

Biography

Biography for children is frequently not documented carefully for accuracy, and it is therefore particularly important
to check the author's credentials—in addition to testing it
against some of the following criteria:

  1. Can you determine if the subject was the author's own
     choice, or was the book contracted for by the pub-
     lisher?

2. Does the author "know" the person and the field?
3. Does the biographee come through as a human being, or as a colorless paragon?
4. Is the dialogue based on imagination, or on diaries, letters, etc.?
5. Have the incidents included in the biography been wisely chosen to give a true portrayal of character and personality?

Science

Here are some special points to check:

1. *readability*—Is the language untechnical enough for the audience?
2. *accuracy*—It is essential to compare books/authorities for authenticity of information.
3. *currency*—In fields where knowledge is rapidly changing, will the book soon be obsolete? Is it already?
4. *illustrations*—Drawings and photographs should be sharp, clear, detailed, positioned, and captioned to aid understanding.
5. *index & bibliography*—A thorough, usable index is a must.
6. Beware of:
   a. *oversimplification*—Concepts should not be confused with facts.
   b. *anthropomorphism*—Treating animals as though they have human characteristics.
   c. *teleology*—Ascribing purpose to anything in the natural environment, e.g., "Squirrels bury acorns so they will have food in winter."

    d. *animism*—Attributing conscious life and spirit to
       material things such as rocks, and plants.

How-to books

Craft, cooking, making things, knitting and other how-to-do-it books should fulfill certain basic criteria:

1. Are the directions clear and complete?
2. Do the instructions include safety precautions?
3. Do the projects encourage creativity, or are they cut-and-dried recipes?
4. Is the finished product worth the effort?

Sports books

Just as sports are full of action, sports books should be exciting, compelling, and dramatic:

1. Does the author create dramatic moments without resorting to clichés?
2. Are statistics used judiciously without bombarding the reader?
3. In how-to sports books, are the skills ones which the intended audience can really attempt?

History

1. Does the book make past eras come alive for the reader?
2. Check the author's accuracy and note any biases.
3. Does the author attempt to present the "facts" from more than one point of view?

BARRY BRICKLIN is a clinical psychologist, associate professor in the Department of Mental Health Sciences at Hahnemann Medical College of Philadelphia, and Co-Book Review Editor of *The Journal of Learning Disabilities*.

21 | Reviewing for Specialized Journals

by BARRY BRICKLIN

IT IS our unspoken rule that reviewers must speak in their own voices. I am opposed to having reviews sound as if they were cut out by the same cookie cutter. Hence, we are likely to accept for publication reviews that may have some shaky sentence construction and even amateur-sounding phrases.

To me, a good review is mainly informative. I look with a jaundiced eye on reviewers as evaluators, and on movie critics, drama critics and the like who think their job is to guard the public's pocketbooks. An "evaluation" certainly belongs in the review, but I like to downplay this aspect.

In selecting books to be reviewed for *The Journal of Learning Disabilities*, we choose first those directly related to the editorial focus of the magazine—learning disabilities —and then those which are related, but of less direct relevance. Sometimes reviews are submitted to us on books that were not "assigned," and if the book is in our field and the review is well written, we accept it. I believe many book review editors would be open to unsolicited reviews, and there is no harm in trying this approach, especially in publications in which the book review columns make up only a small part of the total contents of the magazine. In my experience, journals devoted totally to book reviews are less likely to accept unsolicited reviews. Editors also welcome offers to do reviews, and the best approach is to mail in background material about yourself that establishes your credentials to do specialized reviews for a particular publication.

In order to know what books to assign and to whom, we try to stay informed on new and forthcoming books in our field of learning disabilities and related subjects. We check all advance lists from publishers, and read other books and journals that carry reviews. Once we decide a book should be reviewed in our *Journal,* we go through our lists of reviewers, paying special attention to areas of expertise and previous reliability in producing good reviews on time. When we match a book to the right "expert," the question of reviewer reliability becomes of next major importance. Has the reviewer completed previous assignments within a reasonable length of time? Was it a "good" review? We keep careful records on these points for each reviewer on our list.

If we need a review in a hurry, we naturally give the book to a person we know will do it quickly. If the book to be reviewed is important, we might have to sacrifice speed in order to get an "important" person to review it. Sometimes non-experts tend to be more objective and balanced in the reviews than the experts, and less dogmatic.

In order to find reviewers for *The Journal of Learning Disabilities,* we sometimes put a blurb in the magazine saying that we are on the lookout for reviewers. This is in keeping with our philosophy that you don't have to be an expert to do a good review. This kind of solicitation for new reviewers takes much less time than trying to track down reviewers who turn up in academic sources and publications. We do review carefully the credentials of those who respond to our notice looking for reviewers. We look especially for people well-read in a wide variety of fields. This is of critical importance, since a reviewer even for a specialized journal like ours must be well-rounded, rather than someone who is an expert only in the field of learning disabilities. Well-rounded people are rarely dull and therefore tend to write interesting reviews. They also relate observations from one field to what they know about other fields, and this makes for lively writing and enables one to put observations on the specific book into proper context. The most important qualifications for reviewing books for *The Journal of Learning Disabilities* (and, I am sure, for general publications as well) is to be well-read, to have an interest in all things relating to human beings, and to see the interrelationships among the various disciplines.

The following "Guidelines for Book Reviewers" deal with the specific instructions for writing reviews for our journal:

The *Journal of Learning Disabilities*—a primary scientific and applied publication in its field—discusses programs, techniques, research, and theoretical issues, some controversial, of concern and interest to those involved with helping learning-disabled children. Its reading audience includes representatives from a variety of behavioral and biological disciplines: education, medicine (neurology, ophthalmology, pediatrics, psychiatry, etc.), optometry, psychology, reading, social work and speech.

The Book Review Section endeavors to maintain the level and tone of a professional journal, and should contribute to the overall quality, value and usefulness of the publication. The reader should feel that each book has been reviewed objectively by a professionally competent person, though not necessarily a specialist on learning disabilites. There is no payment for reviews, but reviewers are allowed to keep the books they review.

Specific guidelines

1. The review should state the author's purpose and intended reader audience.

2. It should give a general overview of the content.

3. A statement as to the scientific quality of the publication should be made; e.g., is it based on original research? Does it employ frequent references to the scientific literature? Are references of relatively recent publication?

4. What are the unique qualities of the book (if any)? Does the author offer a new theory? Does he scientifically document an existing theory? Is he qualified to do so?

5. What are the strengths and weaknesses of the book?

6. Do not repeat information already given at the beginning of the review (i.e., name of book, publisher, etc.).

7. Although it is certainly proper to place the author's theoretical position in perspective, and to disagree with that position, avoid using the review to present lengthy dissertations on your own favorite theories. Such arguments belong in regular articles.

8. The final paragraph should present a summary statement of the reviewer's assessment of the book in terms of quality, value, style, and appropriate reader audience.

Format

To cite the book being reviewed, give the title, and name of author(s) or editor(s) in natural order; city in which the publisher is located and name of publisher; year of publication; number of pages; and price (including both cloth and paperback if given).

Example: *Something's Wrong with My Child.* Milton Brutten, Sylvia O. Richardson and Charles Mangel. NY: Harcourt Brace Jovanovich, 1973, 246 pp., $7.50.

Double space all material including extensive quotations. All quoted statements should have a page reference, which is to be enclosed in parentheses within the quotation marks. Example: ". . . (p. 61)"

Reviews should be no less than one page long (approximately 250 words). Reviews of scientific volumes that make a significant contribution to the field may run three to six pages in length (750-1500 words).

Name of reviewer, affiliations, and address should appear at the end of the review. Example:

> John Q. Reviewer
> Research Division
> Smithville Training Center
> Smithville, Tx 76510

Deadlines

The reviewer should submit *two copies* of his book review to the Book Review Editors, no later than six weeks from receipt of the book. If, for any reason, the reviewer does not feel able to review the book, *it should be returned immediately to the Book Review Editors*.

Editing

Minor grammatical and style changes in the manuscript as received from the reviewer may be required during the course of final copy editing prior to publication. The Book Review Editors and the editorial staff of the *Journal* reserve the right to make such changes as they deem necessary according to the style requirements of the *Journal*. If the Editors feel that extensive modification of the review is required, the manuscript and a list of suggestions will be returned to the reviewer for further consideration.

APPENDIX

REFERENCE SHELF

MOST PEOPLE have their own favorite reference books, including a favorite dictionary from among the many available. In addition to such basic volumes as a good dictionary, thesaurus, and book on grammar and usage, the following may be useful to aspiring reviewers.

THE READER'S ENCYCLOPEDIA. *By William Rose Benét. Thomas Y. Crowell Company.*

A basic reference book with thousands of entries of authors, book titles, literary terms, with biographical information, definitions, important literary movements, characters in literary works, myths and legends, and other allusions that are likely to appear in the course of reading.

FAMILIAR QUOTATIONS. *By John Bartlett. Little, Brown.*

The most famous reference work to identify quotations from literature from earliest times through the 1960's.

80 YEARS OF BEST SELLERS 1895-1975. *By Alice Payne Hackett and James Henry Burke. R. R. Bowker Company.*

A list of America's best-selling books from the turn of the century, with a history of best-selling books, arranged by subjects: children's books, cookbooks, crime and suspense, do-it-your-self and gardening, poetry, reference, and religion, supplemented by a title and author index.

LITERARY MARKET PLACE. *R. R. Bowker Company.*

A directory of names and addresses of American book publishers (classified by subject as well as in alphabetical order), book clubs, literary agents, columnists, book reviewers and book reviewing services and syndicates, magazines and other publications, news-papers (arranged by state), radio and television stations, colum-nists, and a host of other useful kinds of information for reviewers. Revised annually.

WHO WON WHAT WHEN. *Compiled by Sandra Lee Stuart. Lyle Stuart, Inc.*

Lists of winners of awards, prizes, honors, scrolls, medals, in-cluding the widely known (Pulitzer, Nobel, Tonys, Grammys, Oscars, etc.) as well as those less familiar, with records running from 1900 to the present.

LITERARY AND LIBRARY PRIZES *9th edition. Edited by Olga S. Weber. R. R. Bowker Company.*

Descriptions of major and minor American and international (including British and Canadian) literary prizes and awards, with the names of the winners from the inception of the prize or award to the present. Periodically revised.

ENCYCLOPEDIA OF MYSTERY AND DETECTION. *Edited by Chris Steinbrunner and Otto Penzler.*

Biographies of principal mystery and detective writers, with information on the motion pictures, plays, radio and television scripts based on the works of major fiction writers in the mystery field; articles on various forms of detective fiction, fic-tional detectives, plot synopses of key works, dates of publication, and checklists of complete works of writers. Illustrated with photo-graphs, motion picture stills, and pictures of actors who starred in films and plays.

A Catalogue of Crime. *By Jacques Barzun and Wendell Hertig Taylor. Harper & Row.*

A reader's guide to the literature of mystery and detective and related genres, with 3500 entries, classical and modern and in between.

Words into Type. *Marjorie E. Skillin and Robert M. Gay. Prentice-Hall, Inc.*

A style manual covering grammar, usage, style, production methods, proofreading (with proofreaders' marks), copy editing, typographical style, manuscript preparation, uses of words, and many other related items, well cross-referenced.

A Manual of Style. *University of Chicago Press.*

A widely used style book, covering the planning of a book, grammar and usage, rules for footnotes and bibliographies, and many other technical topics relating to language and books.

Dictionary of Fictional Characters. *By William Freeman. The Writer, Inc.*

An annotated list of more than 20,000 names of characters in 2,000 classic, semi-classic, and modern works (short stories, novels, poems, plays, operas) by 500 British and American writers.

The Oxford Companion to American Literature. *By James D. Hart. Oxford University Press.*

A one-volume reference book with information about American writers, books, periodicals, newspapers; short essays on American intellectual history and culture, and trends that influenced writing in America; biographies and bibliographies of principal American authors, and summaries and brief descriptions of hunderds of American novels, essays, stories, plays; discussions of literary movements and societies.

The Oxford Companion to English Literature. *Compiled and edited by Paul Harvey. Oxford University Press.*

A one-volume selected listing of English literary works, literary terms, movements, and trends with historical or contemporary importance, authors and the significant dates and activities of their lives, as well as brief descriptions of the nature, content and relative critical importance of the writer and his work. Important references to characters, literary allusions, and literary figures through history are also included.

THE COLUMBIA ENCYCLOPEDIA. *Columbia University Press.*

A comprehensive one-volume reference work, covering a wide range of subjects in all fields of general knowledge: literature, history, art, politics, science, mythology, religious movements, cultural trends, medical discoveries, inventions, and a vast range of other information, described usually in brief entries, but many are discussed in extensive essay form.

BOOK REVIEW DIGEST. *H. W. Wilson Company.*

A cumulative reference available in the reference departments of many public libraries, with quotations from the reviews of works of fiction and nonfiction, as they appeared in major magazines and newspapers. Valuable to a reviewer who wants to check on earlier books by a writer and what various reviewers said about them when they were published.

CONTEMPORARY AUTHORS. *Gale Research Company.*

A continuing, cumulative reference series, frequently updated, with biographies of writers in all fields, as well as prominent media personalities, screenwriters, scriptwriters, well-known newspaper editors; current information about the lives and careers of today's writers, novelists, poets, playwrights, and nonfiction writers—with some 50,000 subjects covered to date. Also included for each author are lists of books published, dates of publication, publishers, and in some cases, the authors' views on writing.

THE WRITER'S HANDBOOK. *The Writer, Inc.*

A collection of 100 articles by leading authors, editors and agents on writing fiction, non-fiction, poetry, stage and television plays, and on the business side of writing. With a complete list, revised annually, of more than 2,500 magazine and book publishers, giving addresses, requirements and payment rates.

LITERARY PRIZE WINNERS

The Winners of the Alfred B. Nobel Prizes for Literature

1901—R. F. A. Sully Prudhomme, French
1902—Th. Mommsen, German
1903—B. Björnson, Norwegian
1904—F. Mistral, French, and J. Echegaray, Spanish
1905—H. Sienkiewicz, Polish
1906—G. Carducci, Italian
1907—R. Kipling, English
1908—R. Eucken, German
1909—Selma Lagerlöf, Swedish (first woman)
1910—P. Heyse, German
1911—M. Maeterlinck, Belgian
1912—G. Hauptmann, German
1913—R. Tagore, Bengali
1914—No award
1915—Romain Rolland, French
1916—Verner von Heidenstam, Swedish
1917—K. Gjellerup and H. Pontoppidan, Danish
1918—No award

1919—Carl Spitteler, Swiss
1920—Knut Hamsun, Norwegian
1921—Anatole France, French
1922—J. Benavente, Spanish
1923—W. B. Yeats, Irish
1924—Wladyslaw Reymont, Polish
1925—G. B. Shaw, English
1926—Grazia Deledda, Italian
1927—Henri Bergson, French
1928—Sigrid Undset, Norwegian
1929—Thomas Mann, German
1930—Sinclair Lewis, American
1931—Erik A. Karlfeldt, Swedish
1932—John Galsworthy, English
1933—Ivan Bunin, Russian
1934—Luigi Pirandello, Italian
1935—No award
1936—Eugene O'Neill, American
1937—Roger M. du Gard, French
1938—Pearl Buck, American
1939—Eemil Sillanpää, Finnish
1940—No award
1941—No award
1942—No award
1943—No award
1944—Johannes V. Jensen, Danish
1945—Gabriela Mistral (pseudonym of Lucila Godoy y Alcayaga),
       Chilean
1946—Hermann Hesse, Swiss
1947—André Gide, French
1948—T. S. Eliot, English
1949—William Faulkner, American
1950—Bertrand Russell, English
1951—Pär Lagerkvist, Swedish
1952—François Mauriac, French
1953—Winston Churchill, English

1954—Ernest Hemingway, American
1955—Halladór Laxness, Icelander
1956—J. R. Jimenez, Spanish
1957—Albert Camus, French
1958—Boris Pasternak, Russian (declined)
1959—Salvatore Quasimodo, Italian
1960—St.-John Perse (pseudonym of Aléxis Léger), French
1961—Ivo Andric, Yugoslavian
1962—John Steinbeck, American
1963—Giorgos Seferis (pseudonym of Giorgos Seferiades), Greek
1964—Jean-Paul Sartre, French (declined)
1965—Mikhail Sholokhov, Russian
1966—S. Y. Agnon, Israeli
      Nelly Sachs, Swedish
1967—Miguel Angel Asturias, Guatemalan
1968—Yasunari Kawabata, Japanese
1969—Samuel Beckett, Irish
1970—Aleksandr Solzhenitsvn, Russian
1971—Pablo Neruda, Chilean
1972—Heinrich Böll, German
1973—Patrick White, Australian
1974—Eyvind Johnson, Swedish
      Harry Martinson, Swedish
1975—Eugenio Montale, Italian
1976—Saul Bellow, American

Pulitzer Prize Winners

Fiction

1918—Ernest Poole, *His Family*
1919—Booth Tarkington, *The Magnificent Ambersons*
1920—No award
1921—Edith Wharton, *The Age of Innocence*
1922—Booth Tarkington, *Alice Adams*

1923—Willa Cather, *One of Ours*
1924—Margaret Wilson, *The Able McLaughlins*
1925—Edna Ferber, *So Big*
1926—Sinclair Lewis, *Arrowsmith* (declined)
1927—Louis Bromfield, *Early Autumn*
1928—Thornton Wilder, *The Bridge of San Luis Rey*
1929—Julia Peterkin, *Scarlet Sister Mary*
1930—Oliver La Farge, *Laughing Boy*
1931—Margaret Ayer Barnes, *Years of Grace*
1932—Pearl Buck, *The Good Earth*
1933—T. S. Stribling, *The Store*
1934—Caroline Miller, *Lamb in His Bosom*
1935—Josephine Winslow Johnson, *Now in November*
1936—H. L. Davis, *Honey in the Horn*
1937—Margaret Mitchell, *Gone with the Wind*
1938—John Phillips Marquand, *The Late George Apley*
1939—Marjorie Kinnan Rawlings, *The Yearling*
1940—John Steinbeck, *The Grapes of Wrath*
1941—No award
1942—Ellen Glasgow, *In This Our Life*
1943—Upton Sinclair, *Dragon's Teeth*
1944—Martin Flavin, *Journey in the Dark*
1945—John Hersey, *A Bell for Adano*
1946—No award
1947—Robert Penn Warren, *All the King's Men*
1948—James A. Michener, *Tales of the South Pacific*
1949—James Gould Cozzens, *Guard of Honor*
1950—A. B. Guthrie, Jr., *The Way West*
1951—Conrad Richter, *The Town*
1952—Herman Wouk, *The Caine Mutiny*
1953—Ernest Hemingway, *The Old Man and the Sea*
1954—No award
1955—William Faulkner, *A Fable*
1956—MacKinlay Kantor, *Andersonville*
1957—No award
1958—James Agee, *A Death in the Family*

1959—Robert Taylor, *Travels of Jamie McPheeters*
1960—Allen Drury, *Advise and Consent*
1961—Harper Lee, *To Kill a Mockingbird*
1962—Edwin O'Connor, *The Edge of Sadness*
1963—William Faulkner, *The Reivers*
1964—No award
1965—Shirley Ann Grau, *Keepers of the House*
1966—Katherine Anne Porter, *Collected Stories*
1967—Bernard Malamud, *The Fixer*
1968—William Styron, *The Confessions of Nat Turner*
1969—N. Scott Momaday, *House Made of Dawn*
1970—Jean Stafford, *Collected Stories*
1971—No award
1972—Wallace Stegner, *Angle of Repose*
1973—Eudora Welty, *The Optimist's Daughter*
1974—No award
1975—Michael Shaara, *The Killer Angels*
1976—Saul Bellow, *Humboldt's Gift*
1977—No award
1978—James Alan McPherson, *Elbow Room*

Poetry

1922—Edwin Arlington Robinson, *Collected Poems*
1923—Edna St. Vincent Millay, *The Ballad of the Harp-Weaver;
        A Few Figs from Thistles; Eight Sonnets*
1924—Robert Frost, *New Hampshire*
1925—Edwin Arlington Robinson, *The Man Who Died Twice*
1926—Amy Lowell, *What's O'Clock?*
1927—Leonora Speyer, *Fiddler's Farewell*
1928—Edwin Arlington Robinson, *Tristram*
1929—Stephen Vincent Benét, *John Brown's Body*
1930—Conrad Aiken, *Selected Poems*
1931—Robert Frost, *Collected Poems*
1932—George Dillon, *The Flowering Stone*
1933—Archibald MacLeish, *Conquistador*

1934—Robert Hillyer, *Collected Verse*
1935—Audrey Wurdemann, *Bright Ambush*
1936—Robert P. Tristram Coffin, *Strange Holiness*
1937—Robert Frost, *A Further Range*
1938—Marya Zaturenska, *Cold Morning Sky*
1939—John Gould Fletcher, *Selected Poems*
1940—Mark Van Doren, *Collected Poems*
1941—Leonard Bacon, *Sunderland Capture*
1942—William Rose Benét, *The Dust Which Is God*
1943—Robert Frost, *A Witness Tree*
1944—Stephen Vincent Benét, *Western Star*
1945—Karl Shapiro, *V-Letter and Other Poems*
1946—No award
1947—Robert Lowell, *Lord Weary's Castle*
1948—W. H. Auden, *The Age of Anxiety*
1949—Peter Viereck, *Terror and Decorum*
1950—Gwendolyn Brooks, *Annie Allen*
1951—Carl Sandburg, *Complete Poems*
1952—Marianne Moore, *Collected Poems*
1953—Archibald MacLeish, *Collected Poems: 1917-1952*
1954—Theodore Roethke, *The Waking*
1955—Wallace Stevens, *Collected Poems*
1956—Elizabeth Bishop, *Poems—North and South*
1957—Richard Wilbur, *Things of This World*
1958—Robert Penn Warren, *Promises: Poems 1954-1956*
1959—Stanley Kunitz, *Selected Poems: 1928-1958*
1960—W. D. Snodgrass, *Heart's Needle*
1961—Phyllis McGinley, *Times Three: Selected Verse from Three
        Decades*
1962—Alan Dugan, *Poems*
1963—William Carlos Williams, *Pictures from Breughel*
1964—Louis Simpson, *At the End of the Open Road*
1965—John Berryman, *Seventy-Seven Dream Songs*
1966—Richard Eberhart, *Selected Poems (1930-1965)*
1967—Anne Sexton, *Live or Die*
1968—Anthony Hecht, *The Hard Hours*

1969—George Oppen, *Of Being Numerous*
1970—Richard Howard, *Untitled Subjects*
1971—W. S. Merwin, *The Carrier of Ladders*
1972—James Wright, *Collected Poems*
1973—Maxine Kumin, *Up Country*
1974—Robert Lowell, *The Dolphin*
1975—Gary Snyder, *Turtle Island*
1976—John Ashbery, *Self-Portrait in a Convex Mirror*
1977—James Merrill, *Divine Comedies*
1978—Howard Nemerov, *Collected Poems*

Biography, Autobiography

1917—Laura E. Richards and Maude Howe Elliott, assisted by
    Florence Howe Hall, *Julia Ward Howe*
1918—William Cabell Bruce, *Benjamin Franklin, Self-Revealed*
1919—Henry Adams *(post obitum)*, *The Education of Henry
    Adams*
1920—Albert J. Beveridge, *The Life of John Marshall*
1921—Edward W. Bok, *The Americanization of Edward Bok*
1922—Hamlin Garland, *A Daughter of the Middle Border*
1923—Burton J. Hendrick, *The Life and Letters of Walter Hines
    Page*
1924—Michael Pupin, *From Immigrant to Inventor*
1925—M. A. DeWolfe Howe, *Barrett Wendell and His Letters*
1926—Dr. Harvey Cushing, *The Life of Sir William Osler*
1927—Emory Holloway, *Whitman*
1928—Charles Edward Russell, *The American Orchestra and
    Theodore Thomas*
1929—Burton J. Hendrick, *The Training of an American*
1930—Marquis James, *The Raven* (Biography of Sam Houston)
1931—Henry James, *Charles W. Eliot*
1932—Henry F. Pringle, *Theodore Roosevelt*
1933—Allan Nevins, *Grover Cleveland*
1934—Tyler Dennett, *John Hay*
1935—Douglas Southall Freeman, *Robert E. Lee*

1936—Ralph Barton Perry, *The Thought and Character of William James*

1937—Allan Nevins, *Hamilton Fish—The Inner History of the Great Administration*

1938—Odell Shepard, *Pedlar's Progress—The Life of Bronson Alcott* and Marquis James, *Andrew Jackson* (Volume One, *The Border Captain* and Volume Two, *Portrait of a President*)

1939—Carl Van Doren, *Benjamin Franklin*

1940—Ray Stannard Baker, *Woodrow Wilson, Life and Letters*

1941—Ola Elizabeth Winslow, *Jonathan Edwards*

1942—Forrest Wilson, *Crusader in Crinoline*

1943—Samuel Eliot Morison, *Admiral of the Ocean Sea*

1944—Carleton Mabee, *The American Leonardo: The Life of Samuel F. B. Morse*

1945—Russel Blaine Nye, *George Bancroft, Brahmin Rebel*

1946—Linnie Marsh Wolfe (*post obitum*), *Son of the Wilderness* (Biography of John Muir)

1947—William Allen White, *The Autobiography of William Allen White*

1948—Margaret Clapp, *Forgotten First Citizen: John Bigelow*

1949—Robert E. Sherwood, *Roosevelt and Hopkins*

1950—Samuel Flagg Bemis, *John Quincy Adams and the Foundations of American Foreign Policy*

1951—Margaret Louise Coit, *John C. Calhoun: American Portrait*

1952—Merlo J. Pusey, *Charles Evans Hughes*

1953—David J. Mays, *Edmund Pendleton 1721-1803*

1954—Charles A. Lindbergh, *The Spirit of St. Louis*

1955—William S. White, *The Taft Story*

1956—Talbot F. Hamlin, *Benjamin Henry Latrobe*

1957—John F. Kennedy, *Profiles in Courage*

1958—Douglass Southall Freeman (deceased 1953), *George Washington, Vols. I-VI;* John Alexander Carroll and Mary Wells Ashworth, *Vol. VII*

1959—Arthur Walworth, *Woodrow Wilson: American Prophet*

1960—Samuel Eliot Morison, *John Paul Jones*

1961—David Donald, *Charles Sumner and the Coming of the Civil War*
1962—No award
1963—Leon Edel, *Henry James: Vol. II, The Conquest of London, 1870-1881; Vol. III, The Middle Years, 1881-1895*
1964—Walter Jackson Bate, *John Keats*
1965—Dr. Ernest Samuels, *Henry Adams*
1966—Arthur M. Schlesinger, Jr., *A Thousand Days*
1967—Justin Kaplan, *Mr. Clemens and Mark Twain*
1968—George F. Kennan, *Memoirs*
1969—Benjamin Lawrence Reid, *The Man From New York: John Quinn and His Friends*
1970—T. Harry Williams, *Huey Long*
1971—Lawrence Thompson, *Robert Frost: The Years of Triumph*
1972—Joseph P. Lash, *Eleanor and Franklin*
1973—W. A. Swanberg, *Luce and His Empire*
1974—Louis Schaeffer, *O'Neill, Son and Artist*
1975—Robert A. Caro, *The Power Broker: Robert Moses and the Fall of New York*
1976—R. W. B. Lewis, *Edith Wharton: A Biography*
1977—John E. Mack, *A Prince of Our Disorder*
1978—Walter Jackson Bate, *Samuel Johnson*

History

1917—J. J. Jusserand, *With Americans of Past and Present Days*
1918—James Ford Rhodes, *A History of the Civil War*
1919—No award
1920—Justin H. Smith, *The War with Mexico*
1921—Rear Admiral William Sowden Sims, *The Victory at Sea*
1922—James T. Adams, *The Founding of New England*
1923—Charles Warren, *The Supreme Court in United States History*
1924—Charles Howard McIlwain, *The American Revolution: A Constitutional Interpretation*
1925—Frederic L. Paxson, *History of the American Frontier*

1926—Edward Channing, *The History of the United States*
1927—Samuel Flagg Bemis, *Pinckney's Treaty*
1928—Vernon Louis Parrington, *Main Currents in American Thought*
1929—Fred A. Shannon, *The Organization and Administration of the Union Army, 1861-65*
1930—Claude H. Van Tyne, *The War of Independence*
1931—Bernadotte E. Schmitt, *The Coming of the War, 1914*
1932—General John J. Pershing, *My Experiences in the World War*
1933—Frederick Jackson Turner, *The Significance of Sections in American History*
1934—Herbert Agar, *The People's Choice*
1935—Charles McLean Andrews, *The Colonial Period of American History*
1936—Andrew C. McLaughlin, *A Constitutional History of the United States*
1937—Van Wyck Brooks, *The Flowering of New England*
1938—Paul Herman Buck, *The Road to Reunion*
1939—Frank Luther Mott, *A History of American Magazines*
1940—Carl Sandburg, *Abraham Lincoln: The War Years*
1941—Marcus Lee Hansen (posthumous), *The Atlantic Migration*
1942—Margaret Leech, *Reveille in Washington*
1943—Esther Forbes, *Paul Revere and the World He Lived In*
1944—Merle Curti, *The Growth of American Thought*
1945—Stephen Bonsal, *Unfinished Business*
1946—Arthur Schlesinger, Jr., *The Age of Jackson*
1947—Dr. James Phinney Baxter III, *Scientists Against Time*
1948—Bernard DeVoto, *Across the Wide Missouri*
1949—Roy F. Nichols, *The Disruption of American Democracy*
1950—O. W. Larkin, *Art and Life in America*
1951—R. Carlyle Buley, *The Old Northwest, Pioneer Period, 1815-1840*
1952—Oscar Handlin, *The Uprooted*
1953—George Dangerfield, *The Era of Good Feelings*
1954—Bruce Catton, *A Stillness at Appomattox*

1955—Paul Horgan, *Great River: The Rio Grande in North American History*

1956—Richard Hofstadter, *The Age of Reform*

1957—George F. Kennan, *Russia Leaves the War*

1958—Bray Hammond, *Banks and Politics in America—From the Revolution to the Civil War*

1959—Leonard D. White, *The Republican Era, 1869-1901*

1960—Margaret Leech, *In the Days of McKinley*

1961—Herbert Feis, *Between War and Peace: The Potsdam Conference*

1962—Lawrence H. Gipson, *The Triumphant Empire, Thunder Clouds Gather in the West*

1963—Constance McLaughlin Green, *Washington, Village and Capital 1800-1878*

1964—Sumner Chilton Powell, *Puritan Village: The Formation of a New England Town*

1965—Irwin Unger, *The Greenback Era*

1966—Perry Miller (*post obitum*), *The Life of the Mind in America: From the Revolution to the Civil War*

1967—William H. Goetzmann, *Exploration and Empire: The Explorer and the Scientist in the Winning of the American West*

1968—Bernard Bailyn, *The Ideological Origins of the American Revolution*

1969—Leonard W. Levy, *Origins of the Fifth Amendment*

1970—Dean Acheson, *Present at the Creation: My Years in the State Department*

1971—James MacGregor Burns, *Roosevelt: The Soldier of Freedom*

1972—Carl N. Degler, *Neither Black Nor White*

1973—Michael Kammen, *People of Paradox: An Inquiry Concerning The Origins of American Civilization*

1974—Daniel J. Boorstin, *The Americans: The Democratic Experience*

1975—Dumas Malone, *Jefferson and His Time*

1976—Paul Horgan, *Lamy of Santa Fe*

1977—David M. Potter, *The Impending Crisis*
1978—Alfred D. Chandler, Jr., *The Invisible Hand: The Managerial Revolution in American Business*

General Nonfiction

1962—Theodore White, *The Making of the President, 1960*
1963—Barbara W. Tuchman, *The Guns of August*
1964—Richard Hofstadter, *Anti-Intellectualism in American Life*
1965—Howard Mumford Jones, *O Strange New World*
1966—Edwin Way Teale, *Wandering Through Winter*
1967—David Brion Davis, *The Problem of Slavery in Western Culture*
1968—Will and Ariel Durant, *Rousseau and Revolution*
1969—René Jules Dubos, *So Human an Animal*
Norman Mailer, *The Armies of the Night*
1970—Erik H. Erikson, *Gandhi's Truth*
1971—John Toland, *The Rising Sun*
1972—Barbara W. Tuchman, *Stilwell and the American Experience in China, 1911-1945*
1973—Robert Coles, *Children of Crisis, Vols. II and III*
Frances FitzGerald, *Fire in the Lake*
1974—Ernest Becker, *The Denial of Death*
1975—Annie Dillard, *Pilgrim at Tinker Creek*
1976—Robert N. Butler, *Why Survive? Being Old in America*
1977—William W. Warner, *Beautiful Swimmers: Crabs & the Chesapeake Bay*
1978—Carl Sagan, *The Dragons of Eden*

Drama

1918—Jesse Lynch Williams, *Why Marry?*
1919—No award
1920—Eugene O'Neill, *Beyond the Horizon*
1921—Zona Gale, *Miss Lulu Bett*
1922—Eugene O'Neill, *Anna Christie*

1923—Owen Davis, *Icebound*
1924—Hatcher Hughes, *Hell-Bent for Heaven*
1925—Sidney Howard, *They Knew What They Wanted*
1926—George Kelly, *Craig's Wife*
1927—Paul Green, *In Abraham's Bosom*
1928—Eugene O'Neill, *Strange Interlude*
1929—Elmer Rice, *Street Scene*
1930—Marc Connelly, *The Green Pastures*
1931—Susan Glaspell, *Alison's House*
1932—George S. Kaufman, Morrie Ryskind, and Ira Gershwin, *Of Thee I Sing*
1933—Maxwell Anderson, *Both Your Houses*
1934—Sidney Kingsley, *Men in White*
1935—Zoë Akins, *The Old Maid*
1936—Robert E. Sherwood, *Idiot's Delight*
1937—George S. Kaufman and Moss Hart, *You Can't Take It with You*
1938—Thornton Wilder, *Our Town*
1939—Robert E. Sherwood, *Abe Lincoln in Illinois*
1940—William Saroyan, *The Time of Your Life* (declined)
1941—Robert E. Sherwood, *There Shall Be No Night*
1942—No award
1943—Thornton Wilder, *The Skin of Our Teeth*
1944—No award
1945—Mary Chase, *Harvey*
1946—Howard Lindsay and Russel Crouse, *State of the Union*
1947—No award
1948—Tennessee Williams, *A Streetcar Named Desire*
1949—Arthur Miller, *Death of a Salesman*
1950—Richard Rogers, Oscar Hammerstein II, and Joshua Logan, *South Pacific*
1951—No award
1952—Joseph Kramm, *The Shrike*
1953—William Inge, *Picnic*
1954—John Patrick, *Teahouse of the August Moon*
1955—Tennessee Williams, *Cat on a Hot Tin Roof*

1956—Frances Goodrich and Albert Hackett, *The Diary of Anne Frank*

1957—Eugene O'Neill, *Long Day's Journey Into Night*

1958—Ketti Frings, *Look Homeward, Angel*

1959—Archibald MacLeish, *J. B.*

1960—George Abbott, Jerome Weidman, Sheldon Harnick and Jerry Bock, *Fiorello!*

1961—Tad Mosel, *All the Way Home*

1962—Frank Loesser and Abe Burrows, *How to Succeed in Business without Really Trying*

1963—No award

1964—No award

1965—Frank Gilroy, *The Subject Was Roses*

1966—No award

1967—Edward Albee, *A Delicate Balance*

1968—No award

1969—Howard Sackler, *The Great White Hope*

1970—Charles Gordone, *No Place To Be Somebody*

1971—Paul Zindel, *The Effect of Gamma Rays on Man-in-the-Moon Marigolds*

1972—No award

1973—Jason Miller, *That Championship Season*

1974—No award

1975—Edward Albee, *Seascape*

1976—Michael Bennett, James Kirkwood, Nicholas Dante, Marvin Hamlisch, Edward Kleban, *A Chorus Line*

1977—Michael Cristofer, *The Shadow Box*

1978—Donald L. Coburn, *The Gin Game*

The National Book Awards

The National Book Awards are presented annually for books which five panels of judges consider the most distinguished books written by American citizens and published in the United States in the preceding year.

Fiction

1950—Nelson Algren, *The Man with the Golden Arm*
1951—William Faulkner, *Collected Stories*
      Special Citation to Brendan Gill, *The Trouble of One House*
1952—James Jones, *From Here to Eternity*
1953—Ralph Ellison, *Invisible Man*
1954—Saul Bellow, *The Adventures of Augie March*
1955—William Faulkner, *A Fable*
1956—John O'Hara, *Ten North Frederick*
1957—Wright Morris, *The Field of Vision*
1958—John Cheever, *The Wapshot Chronicle*
1959—Bernard Malamud, *The Magic Barrel*
1960—Philip Roth, *Goodbye, Columbus*
1961—Conrad Richter, *The Waters of Kronos*
1962—Walker Percy, *The Moviegoer*
1963—J. F. Powers, *Morte D'Urban*
1964—John Updike, *The Centaur*
1965—Saul Bellow, *Herzog*
1966—Katherine Anne Porter, *Collected Stories*
1967—Bernard Malamud, *The Fixer*
1968—Thornton Wilder, *The Eighth Day*
1969—Jerzy Kosinski, *Steps*
1970—Joyce Carol Oates, *Them*
1971—Saul Bellow, *Mr. Sammler's Planet*
1972—Flannery O'Connor, *The Complete Stories*
1973—John Barth, *Chimera*
      John Wiliams, *Augustus*
1974—Thomas Pynchon, *Gravity's Rainbow*
      Isaac Bashevis Singer, *A Crown of Feathers and Other Stories*
1975—Robert Stone, *Dog Soldiers*
      Thomas Williams, *The Hair of Harold Roux*
1976—William Gaddis, *JR*
1977—Wallace E. Stegner, *The Spectator Bird*
1978—Mary Lee Settle, *Blood Tie*

Poetry

1950—William Carlos Williams, *Paterson III* and *Selected Poems*
1951—Wallace Stevens, *The Auroras of Autumn*
1952—Marianne Moore, *Collected Poems*
1953—Archibald MacLeish, *Collected Poems, 1917-1952*
1954—Conrad Aiken, *Collected Poems*
1955—Wallace Stevens, *The Collected Poems of Wallace Stevens*
         Special citation to E. E. Cummings, *Poems: 1923-1954*
1956—W. H. Auden, *The Shield of Achilles*
1957—Richard Wilbur, *Things of This World*
1958—Robert Penn Warren, *Promises: Poems 1954-1956*
1959—Theodore Roethke, *Words for the Wind*
1960—Robert Lowell, *Life Studies*
1961—Randall Jarrell, *The Woman at the Washington Zoo*
1962—Alan Dugan, *Poems*
1963—William Stafford, *Traveling Through the Dark*
1964—John Crowe Ransom, *Selected Poems*
1965—Theodore Roethke (posthumous), *The Far Field*
1966—James Dickey, *Buckdancer's Choice*
1967—James Merrill, *Nights and Days*
1968—Robert Bly, *The Light Around the Body*
1969—John Berryman, *His Toy, His Dream, His Rest*
1970—Elizabeth Bishop, *The Complete Poems*
1971—Mona Van Duyn, *To See, To Take*
1972—Frank O'Hara, *The Collected Poems*
         Howard Moss, *Selected Poems*
1973—A. R. Ammons, *Collected Poems: 1951-1971*
1974—Allen Ginsberg, *The Fall of America: Poems of These
         States, 1965-1971*
         Adrienne Rich, *Diving Into the Wreck: Poems, 1971-72*
1975—Marilyn Hacker, *Presentation Piece*
1976—John Ashbery, *Self-Portrait in a Convex Mirror*
1977—Richard Eberhart, *Collected Poems, 1930-1976*
1978—Howard Nemerov, *The Collected Poems*

Nonfiction

1950—Ralph L. Rusk, *Ralph Waldo Emerson*
1951—Newton Arvin, *Herman Melville*
1952—Rachel Carson, *The Sea Around Us*
1953—Bernard DeVoto, *The Course of Empire*
1954—Bruce Catton, *A Stillness at Appomattox*
1955—Joseph Wood Krutch, *The Measure of Man*
1956—Herbert Kubly, *American in Italy*
1957—George F. Kennan, *Russia Leaves the War*
1958—Catherine Drinker Bowen, *The Lion and the Throne*
1959—J. Christopher Herold, *Mistress to an Age*
1960—Richard Ellman, *James Joyce*
1961—William L. Shirer, *The Rise and Fall of the Third Reich*
1962—Lewis Mumford, *The City in History*
1963—Leon Edel, *Henry James: The Conquest of London; Henry James: The Middle Years*
1964—*Arts and Letters:* Aileen Ward, *John Keats: The Making of a Poet*
    History and Biography: William H. McNeill, *The Rise of the West*
    Science, Philosophy, and Religion: Christopher Tunnard and Boris Pushkarev, *Man-Made America: Chaos or Control?*
1965—*Arts and Letters:* Eleanor Clark, *The Oysters of Locmariaquer*
    History and Biography: Louis Fischer, *The Life of Lenin*
    Science, Philosophy, and Religion: Norbert Wiener (posthumous), *God and Golem, Inc.*
1966—*Arts and Letters:* Janet Flanner (Genêt), *Paris Journal, 1944-1965*
    History and Biography: Arthur M. Schlesinger, Jr., *A Thousand Days*
1967—*Arts and Letters:* Justin Kaplan, *Mr. Clemens and Mark Twain*
    History and Biography: Peter Gay, *The Enlightenment: An Interpretation*
    Science, Philosophy, and Religion: Oscar Lewis, *La Vida*

1968—*Arts and Letters:* William Troy, *Selected Essays*
    History and Biography: George F. Kennan, *Memoirs*
    Science, Philosophy, and Religion: Jonathan Kozol, *Death at an Early Age*

1969—*Arts and Letters:* Norman Mailer, *The Armies of the Night*
    History and Biography: Winthrop D. Jordan, *White Over Black*
    Sciences: Robert J. Lifton, *Death in Life: Survivors of Hiroshima*

1970—*Arts and Letters:* Lillian Hellman, *An Unfinished Woman*
    History and Biography: T. Harry Williams, *Huey Long*
    Philosophy and Religion: Erik H. Erikson, *Gandhi's Truth*

1971—*Arts and Letters:* Francis Steegmuller, *Cocteau*
    History and Biography: James MacGregor Burns, *Roosevelt: The Soldier of Freedom*
    Sciences: Raymond Phineas Stearns, *Science in the British Colonies of America*

1972—*Arts and Letters:* Charles Rosen, *The Classical Style: Haydn, Mozart, Beethoven*
    History: Allan Nevins, *Ordeal of the Union Series: The War for the Union, Vol. VII, Vol. VIII*
    Science: George L. Small, *The Blue Whale*
    Philosophy: Martin E. Marty, *Righteous Empire: The Protestant Experience in America*
    Contemporary Affairs: Stewart Brand, *The Last Whole Earth Catalog*

1973—*Arts and Letters:* Arthur M. Wilson, *Diderot*
    History: Isaiah Trunk, *Judenrat: The Jewish Councils in Eastern Europe Under Nazi Occupation*
    Robert Manson Myers, *The Children of Pride: A True Story of Georgia and the Civil War*
    Sciences: George B. Schaller, *The Serengeti Lion*
    Philosophy: Syndey E. Ahlstrom, *A Religious History of The American People*
    Contemporary Affairs: Frances FitzGerald, *Fire in the Lake*

1974—*Arts and Letters:* Pauline Kael, *Deeper Into Movies*
    History: John Clive, *Macaulay*
    Sciences: S. E. Luria, *Life: The Unfinished Experiment*
    Philosophy and Religion: Maurice Natanson, *Edmund Husserl*
    Contemporary Affairs: Murray Kempton, *The Briar Patch*
1975—*Arts and Letters:* Roger Shattuck, *Marcel Proust*
    History: Bernard Bailyn, *The Ordeal of Thomas Hutchinson*
    Philosophy and Religion: Robert Nozick, *Anarchy, State & Utopia*
    Sciences: Silvano Arieti, *Interpretations of Schizophrenia*
    Lewis Thomas, *The Lives of a Cell: Notes of a Biology Watcher*
    Contemporary Affairs: Theodore Rosengarten, *All God's Dangers*
1976—*Arts and Letters:* Paul Fussell, *The Great War and Modern Memory*
    History: David Brion Davis, *The Problem of Slavery in the Age of Revolution*
    Contemporary Affairs: Michael J. Arlen, *Passage to Ararat*
1977—*History:* Irving Howe, *World of Our Fathers*
    Contemporary Thought: Bruno Bettelheim, *The Uses of Enchantment*
    Special Award: Alex Haley, *Roots*
1978—*History:* David McCullough, *The Path Between The Seas*
    Contemporary Thought: Gloria Emerson, *Winners and Losers*

Children's Literature

1969—Meindert DeJong, *Journey From Peppermint Street*
1970—Isaac Bashevis Singer, *A Day of Pleasure: Stories of a Boy Growing Up in Warsaw*
1971—Lloyd Alexander, *The Marvelous Misadventures of Sebastian*

1972—Donald Barthelme, *The Slightly Irregular Fire Engine or the Hithering Thithering Djinn*
1973—Ursula LeGuin, *The Farthest Shore*
1974—Eleanor Cameron, *The Court of the Stone Children*
1975—Virginia Hamilton, *M. C. Higgins the Great*
1976—Walter D. Edmonds, *Bert Breen's Barn*
1977—Katherine W. Paterson, *The Master Puppeteer*
1978—Judith and Herbert Kohl, *The View from the Oak*

Biography

For listings prior to 1972, see *Nonfiction: History and Biography.*

1972—Joseph P. Lash, *Eleanor and Franklin*
1973—James Thomas Flexner, *George Washington*
1974—Douglas Day, *Malcolm Lowry: A Biography*
1975—Richard B. Sewall, *The Life of Emily Dickinson*
1976—No award
1977—W. A. Swanberg, *Norman Thomas: The Last Idealist*
1978—W. Jackson Bate, *Samuel Johnson*

Newbery Medal Awards

The John Newbery Medal is awarded annually for the most distinguished contribution to literature for American children.

	Title	Author
1922	*Story of Mankind*	Hendrik van Loon
1923	*Voyages of Dr. Dolittle*	Hugh Lofting
1924	*Dark Frigate*	Charles B. Hawes
1925	*Tales from Silver Lands*	Charles J. Finger
1926	*Shen of the Sea*	Arthur B. Chrisman
1927	*Smoky, the Cowhorse*	Will James
1928	*Gay-Neck*	Dhan Gopal Mukerji
1929	*Trumpeter of Krakow*	Eric P. Kelly
1930	*Hitty*	Rachel Field
1931	*The Cat Who Went to Heaven*	Elizabeth J. Coatsworth

	Title	Author
1932	*Waterless Mountain*	Laura Armer
1933	*Young Fu of the Upper Yangtze*	Elizabeth F. Lewis
1934	*Invincible Louisa*	Cornelia Meigs
1935	*Dobry*	Monica Shannon
1936	*Caddie Woodlawn*	Carol R. Brink
1937	*Roller Skates*	Ruth Sawyer
1938	*White Stag*	Kate Seredy
1939	*Thimble Summer*	Elizabeth Enright
1940	*Daniel Boone*	James Daugherty
1941	*Call It Courage*	Armstrong Sperry
1942	*Matchlock Gun*	Walter D. Edmonds
1943	*Adam of the Road*	Elizabeth Janet Gray
1944	*Johnny Tremain*	Esther Forbes
1945	*Rabbit Hill*	Robert Lawson
1946	*Strawberry Girl*	Lois Lenski
1947	*Miss Hickory*	Carolyn Sherwin Bailey
1948	*Twenty-One Balloons*	William Pène du Bois
1949	*King of the Wind*	Marguerite Henry
1950	*Door in the Wall*	Marguerite de Angeli
1951	*Amos Fortune, Free Man*	Elizabeth Yates
1952	*Ginger Pye*	Eleanor Estes
1953	*Secret of the Andes*	Ann Nolan Clark
1954	*. . . And Now Miguel*	Joseph Krumgold
1955	*Wheel on the School*	Meindert DeJong
1956	*Carry On, Mr. Bowditch*	Jean Lee Latham
1957	*Miracles on Maple Hill*	Virginia Sorensen
1958	*Rifles for Watie*	Harold Keith
1959	*Witch of Blackbird Pond*	Elizabeth George Speare
1960	*Onion John*	Joseph Krumgold
1961	*Island of the Blue Dolphins*	Scott O'Dell
1962	*The Bronze Bow*	Elizabeth George Speare
1963	*A Wrinkle in Time*	Madeleine L'Engle

	Title	Author
1964	*It's Like This, Cat*	Emily Neville
1965	*Shadow of a Bull*	Maia Wojciechowska
1966	*I, Juan de Pareja*	Elizabeth Borton de Trevino
1967	*Up a Road Slowly*	Irene Hunt
1968	*From the Mixed-Up Files of Mrs. Basil E. Frankweiler*	E. L. Konigsburg
1969	*High King*	Lloyd Alexander
1970	*Sounder*	William H. Armstrong
1971	*Summer of the Swans*	Betsy Byars
1972	*Mrs. Frisby and the Rats of NIMH*	Robert C. O'Brien
1973	*Julie of the Wolves*	Jean Craighead George
1974	*Slave Dancer*	Paula Fox
1975	*M. C. Higgins the Great*	Virginia Hamilton
1976	*The Grey King*	Susan Cooper
1977	*Roll of Thunder, Hear My Cry*	Mildred D. Taylor
1978	*Bridge to Terabithia*	Katherine Paterson

Caldecott Medal Awards

The Caldecott Medal is awarded to the illustrator of the most distinguished American picture book for children.

	Title	Author and Illustrator
1938	*Animals of the Bible*	Dorothy Lathrop
1939	*Mei Li*	Thomas Handforth
1940	*Abraham Lincoln*	Ingri and Edgar d'Aulaire
1941	*They Were Strong and Good*	Robert Lawson
1942	*Make Way for Ducklings*	Robert McCloskey
1943	*Little House*	Virginia Burton
1944	*Many Moons*	James Thurber and Louis Slobodkin

	Title	Author and Illustrator
1945	*Prayer for a Child*	Rachel Field and Elizabeth Orton Jones
1946	*Rooster Crows*	Maud and Miska Petersham
1947	*The Little Island*	Golden MacDonald and Leonard Weisgard
1948	*White Snow, Bright Snow*	Alvin Tresselt and Roger Duvoisin
1949	*The Big Snow*	Berta and Elmer Hader
1950	*Song of the Swallows*	Leo Politi
1951	*The Egg Tree*	Katherine Milhous
1952	*Finders Keepers*	Will and Nicolas
1953	*Biggest Bear*	Lynd Ward
1954	*Madeline's Rescue*	Ludwig Bemelmans
1955	*Cinderella*	Marcia Brown
1956	*A Frog Went A'Courtin'*	John Langstaff and Feodor Rojankovsky
1957	*A Tree Is Nice*	Janice May Udry and Marc Simont
1958	*Time of Wonder*	Robert McCloskey
1959	*Chanticleer and the Fox*	Barbara Cooney
1960	*Nine Days to Christmas*	Maire Hall Ets and Aurora Labastida
1961	*Baboushka and the Three Kings*	Ruth Robbins and Nicolas Sidjakov
1962	*Once a Mouse*	Marcia Brown
1963	*The Snowy Day*	Ezra Jack Keats
1964	*Where the Wild Things Are*	Maurice Sendak
1965	*May I Bring a Friend?*	Beatrice de Regniers and Beni Montresor
1966	*Always Room for One More*	Sorche Nic Leodhas and Nonny Hogrogian
1967	*Sam, Bangs, and Moonshine*	Evaline Ness
1968	*Drummer Hoff*	Barbara and Ed Emberly

	Title	Author and Illustrator
1969	*The Fool of the World and the Flying Ship*	Arthur Ransome and Uri Shulevitz
1970	*Sylvester and the Magic Pebble*	William Steig
1971	*A Story, A Story*	Gail E. Haley
1972	*One Fine Day*	Nonny Hogrogian
1973	*The Funny Little Woman*	Arlene Mosel and Blair Lent
1974	*Duffy and the Devil*	Harve and Margot Zemach
1975	*Arrow to the Sun*	Gerald McDermott
1976	*Why Mosquitoes Buzz in People's Ears*	Verna Aardema and Leo and Diane Dillon
1977	*Ashanti to Zulu*	Margaret Musgrove and Leo and Diana Dillon
1978	*Noah's Ark*	Peter Spier

National Book Critics Circle Awards

The National Book Critics Circle—book editors and reviewers—presents awards annually for the best books published during the preceding year.

Fiction

1975—E. L. Doctorow, *Ragtime*
1976—John Gardner, *October Light*
1977—Toni Morrison, *Song of Solomon*

Poetry

1975—John Ashbery, *Self-Portrait in a Convex Mirror*
1976—Elizabeth Bishop, *Geography III*
1977—Robert Lowell, *Day by Day*

General Nonfiction

1975—R. W. B. Lewis, *Edith Wharton*
1976—Maxine Hong Kingston, *The Woman Warrior*
1977—W. Jackson Bate, *Samuel Johnson*

Criticism

1975—Paul Fussell, *The Great War and Modern Memory*
1976—Bruno Bettelheim, *The Uses of Enchantment*
1977—Susan Sontag, *On Photography*

Edgar Allan Poe Awards

The "Edgars" are presented annually by the Mystery Writers of America for the best works of mystery in several categories.

Best Novel

1954—Charlotte Jay, *Beat Not the Bones*
1955—Ira Levin, *A Kiss Before Dying*
1955—Raymond Chandler, *The Long Goodbye*
1956—Margaret Millar, *Beast in View*
1957—Charlotte Armstrong, *A Dram of Poison*
1958—Ed Lacy, *Room to Swing*
1959—Stanley Ellin, *The Eighth Circle*
1960—Celia Fremlin, *The Hours Before Dawn*
1961—Julian Symons, *Progress of a Crime*
1962—Ellis Peters, *Death and the Joyful Woman*
1963—Eric Ambler, *The Light of Day*
1964—John Le Carré, *The Spy Who Came in From the Cold*
1965—Adam Hall, *The Quiller Memorandum*
1966—Nicolas Freeling, *King of the Rainy Country*
1967—Donald Westlake, *God Save the Mark*
1968—Jeffrey Hudson, *A Case of Need*
1969—Dick Francis, *Forfeit*
1970—Maj Sjowall and Per Wahlöö, *The Laughing Policeman*
1971—Frederick Forsyth, *Day of the Jackal*
1972—Warren Kiefer, *The Lingala Code*
1973—Tony Hillerman, *The Dance of the Dead*
1974—Jon Cleary, *Peter's Pence*
1975—Brian Garfield, *Hopscotch*
1976—Robert Parker, *Promised Land*
1977—William H. Hallahan, *Catch Me, Kill Me*

Best First Novel

1946—Julius Fast, *Watchful at Night*
1947—Helen Eustis, *The Horizontal Man*
1948—Frederic Brown, *The Fabulous Clipjoint*
1949—Mildred Davis, *The Room Upstairs*
1950—Alan Breen, *What a Body*
1951—Thomas Walsh, *Nightmare in Manhattan*
1952—Mary McMullen, *Strangle Hold*
1953—William Campbell Gault, *Don't Cry for Me*
1954—Ira Levin, *A Kiss Before Dying*
1955—Jean Potts, *Go, Lovely Rose*
1956—Lane Kauffman, *The Perfectionist*
1957—Douglas McNutt Douglas, *Rebecca's Pride*
1958—William R. Weeks, *Knock and Wait a While*
1959—Richard Martin Stern, *The Bright Road to Fear*
1960—Henry Slesar, *The Grey Flannel Shroud*
1961—John Holbrooke Vance, *The Man in the Cage*
1962—Suzanne Blanc, *The Green Stone*
1963—Robert L. Fish, *The Fugitive*
1964—Cornelius Hirschberg, *Florentine Finish*
1965—Harry Kemelman, *Friday the Rabbi Slept Late*
1966—John Ball, *In the Heat of the Night*
1967—Ross Thomas, *The Cold War Swap*
1968—Michael Collins, *Act of Fear*
1969—Joe Gores, *A Time of Predators*
1970—Lawrence Sanders, *The Anderson Tapes*
1971—A. H. Z. Carr, *Finding Maubee*
1972—R. H. Shimer, *Squaw Point*
1973—Paul E. Erdman, *The Billion Dollar Sure Thing*
1974—Gregory MacDonald, *Fletch*
1975—Rex Burns, *The Alvarez Journal*
1976—James Patterson, *The Thomas Berryman Number*
1977—Robert Ross, *A French Finish*

Best Juvenile Mystery

1960—Phyllis A. Whitney, *The Mystery of the Haunted Pool*

1961—Edward Fenton, *The Phantom of Walkaway Hill*
1962—Scott Corbett, *Cutlass Island*
1963—Phyllis A. Whitney, *The Mystery of the Hidden Hand*
1964—Marcella Thum, *The Mystery at Crane's Landing*
1965—Leon Ware, *The Mystery of 22 East*
1966—Kin Platt, *Sinbad and Me*
1967—Gretchen Sprague, *Signpost to Terror*
1968—Virginia Hamilton, *The House of Dies Drear*
1969—Winifred Finlay, *Danger at Black Dyke*
1970—John Rowe Townsend, *The Intruder*
1971—Joan Aiken, *Night Fall*
1972—Robb White, *Death Watch*
1973—Jay Bennett, *The Long Black Coat*
1974—Jay Bennett, *The Dangling Witness*
1975—Robert C. O'Brien, *Z for Zachariah*
1976—Richard Peck, *Are You in the House Alone?*
1977—Eloise Jarvis McGraw, *A Really Weird Summer*

Fact Crime

1947—Edward D. Radin, *Twelve Against the Law*
1948—Marie Rodell, Editorship of 1948 volume, *Regional Murders*
1949—Joseph Henry Jackson, *Bad Company*
1950—Edward D. Radin, Editorship of *Detective* Magazine
1951—St. Clair McKelway, *True Tales From the Annals of Crime
        and Rascality*
1952—Erle Stanley Gardner, *Court of Last Resort*
1953—John Bartlow Martin, *Why Did They Kill?*
1954—Charles Boswell and Lewis Thompson, *The Girl With the
        Scarlet Brand*
1955—Manly Wade Wellman, *Dead and Gone*
1956—Charles and Louise Samuels, *Night Fell on Georgia*
1957—Harold R. Danforth and James D. Horan, *The D.A.'s Man*
1958—Wenzell Brown, *They Died in the Chair*
1959—Thomas Gallagher, *Fire at Sea*
1960—Miriam Allen deFord, *The Overbury Affair*
1961—Barrett Prettymen, *Death and the Supreme Court*

1962—Francis Russell, *Tragedy in Dedham*
1963—Gerold Frank, *The Deed*
1964—Anthony Lewis, *Gideon's Trumpet*
1965—Truman Capote, *In Cold Blood*
1966—Gerold Frank, *The Boston Strangler*
1967—Victoria Lincoln, *A Private Disgrace*
1968—John Walsh, *Poe the Detective*
1969—Herbert B. Ehrmann, *The Case That Will Not Die*
1970—Mildred Savage, *A Great Fall*
1971—Sandor Frankel, *Beyond a Reasonable Doubt*
1972—Stephen Fay, Lewis Chester, and Magnus Linkletter, *Hoax*
1973—Barbara Levy, *Legacy of Death*
1974—Vincent Bugliosi and Curt Gentry, *Helter Skelter*
1975—Tom Wicker, *A Time to Die*
1976—Thomas Thompson, *Blood and Money*
1977—George Jonas and Barbara Amiel, *By Persons Unknown*

Hugo Awards

"Hugo" Awards, originally called Science Fiction Achievement Awards, are given by the annual World Science Fiction Convention.

1953—Alfred Bester, *The Demolished Man*
1954—No award
1955—Mark Clifton and Frank Riley, *They'd Rather Be Right*
1956—Robert Heinlein, *Double Star*
1957—No award
1958—Fritz Lieber, *The Big Time*
1959—James Blish, *A Case of Conscience*
1960—Robert Heinlein, *Starship Troopers*
1961—Walter M. Miller, Jr., *A Canticle for Liebowitz*
1962—Robert Heinlein, *Stranger in a Strange Land*
1963—Philip K. Dick, *The Man in the High Castle*
1964—Clifford D. Simak, *Way Station*
1965—Fritz Lieber, *The Wanderer*

1966—Roger Zelazny, . . . *And Call Me Conrad*
        Frank Herbert, *Dune*
1967—Robert Heinlein, *The Moon is a Harsh Mistress*
1968—Roger Zelazny, *Lord of Light*
1969—John Brunner, *Stand on Zanzibar*
1970—Ursula K. LeGuin, *The Left Hand of Darkness*
1971—Larry Niven, *Ringworld*
1972—Philip Jose Farmer, *To Your Scattered Bodies Go*
1973—Isaac Asimov, *The Gods Themselves*
1974—Arthur C. Clarke, *Rendezvous With Rama*
1975—Ursula K. LeGuin, *The Dispossessed*
1976—Joe Haldeman, *The Forever War*
1977—Kate Wilhelm, *Where Late the Sweet Birds Sang*

Nebula Awards

The Nebula Awards are presented by the Science Fiction Writers of America for the best science fiction novel published during the preceding year.

1965—Frank Herbert, *Dune*
1966—Samuel Delany *Babel 17*
        Daniel Keyes, *Flowers for Algernon*
1967—Samuel Delany, *The Einstein Intersection*
1968—Alexie Panshin, *Rite of Passage*
1969—Ursula K. LeGuin, *The Left Hand of Darkness*
1970—Larry Niven, *Ringworld*
1971—Robert Silverberg, *A Time of Changes*
1972—Isaac Asimov, *The Gods Themselves*
1973—Arthur C. Clarke, *Rendezvous With Rama*
1974—Ursula K. LeGuin, *The Dispossessed*
1975—Joe Haldeman, *The Forever War*
1976—Frederik Pohl, *Man Plus*
1977—Frederik Pohl, *Gateway*